Connected Sociologies

THEORY FOR A GLOBAL AGE

Series Editor: Gurminder K. Bhambra, University of Warwick, UK.

Editorial Board: Michael Burawoy (University of California Berkeley, USA), Neera Chandhoke, (University of Delhi, India) Robin Cohen (University of Oxford, UK), Peo Hansen (Linköping University, Sweden) John Holmwood (University of Nottingham, UK), Walter Mignolo (Duke University, USA), Emma Porio (Ateneo de Manila University, Philippines), Boaventura de Sousa Santos (University of Coimbra, Portugal).

Globalization is widely viewed as the current condition of the world, only recently come into being. There is little engagement with its long histories and how these histories continue to have an impact on current social, political, and economic configurations and understandings. Theory for a Global Age takes 'the global' as the already-always existing condition of the world and one that should have informed analysis in the past as well as informing analysis for the present and future. The series is not about globalization as such, but, rather, it addresses the impact a properly critical reflection on 'the global' might have on disciplines and different fields within the social sciences and humanities. It asks how we might understand our present and future differently if we start from a critical examination of the idea of the global as a political and interpretive device; and what consequences this would have for reconstructing our understandings of the past, including our disciplinary pasts.

Each book in the series focuses on a particular theoretical issue or topic of empirical controversy and debate, addressing theory in a more comprehensive and interconnected manner in the process. With books commissioned from scholars from across the globe, the series explores understandings of the global – and global understandings – from diverse viewpoints. The series will be available in print, in eBook format and free online, through a Creative Commons licence, aiming to encourage academic engagement on a broad geographical scale and to further the reach of the debates and dialogues that the series develops.

Contents

Series Foreword

As the first volume in this series, Gurminder K. Bhambra's *Connected Sociologies* bears a special responsibility in providing the intellectual compass for the series as a whole. She does this in a challenging and engaging way. Her starting point is that, despite its ambitions, sociology has remained a fragmented discipline. She sees comparative and historical sociology, and more recent attempts to adumbrate a global sociology, as partial and incomplete. Despite meetings of the International Sociological Association in India, Mexico and South Africa and notwithstanding the growth of the discipline all over the world, there is still a sense in which western sociology has remained hegemonic and continues to be indifferent to dissident and peripheral voices. Sociologists from the rest of the world are simply not connecting with colleagues in the west as equal epistemic communities.

Bhambra makes a convincing case that one root of this problem lies in the abject failure of sociology and anthropology to engage seriously with each other. As she affirms, it is no longer possible to separate out the subject domains of these two cognate disciplines. Indeed, their initial separation is illustrative of the problem. If the very heart of modernity was mercantile capitalism, colonialism and imperialism, to side-line empire from the subject of sociology was a significant and far-reaching historical distortion. Such a distortion was later magnified, so I understand her argument, in Marx's notion of successive modes of production, by Rostow's 'stages theory', and in the dominant versions of 'civilizational analysis'. The normative direction of movement was nearly always from *them* (the peripheral, marginal, backward, primitive, poor, underdeveloped) to *us* (enjoying the opposite conditions).

For Bhambra, the 'us' is Europe or Europe transplanted to the USA, and even when universal values and the cosmopolitan spirit are evoked, the 'us' remains largely inviolate. In this respect it is notable that Habermas and Beck find their embryonic cosmopolitanism in the European Union. This is self-limiting in Bhambra's view and, incidentally, also rather over-optimistic in the light of the rabid forms of nationalism rearing their ugly heads in so many European countries. She accepts that Wallerstein (in his world system and other writings) and Mann (in his ambitious extension of Weber) made major attempts to define a globally-based sociology, but neither escapes Bhambra's critique that they are working from the inner ring to the outer circle and using a method (delineating ideal-types) which, she argues, is unsatisfactory.

What then is Gurminder K. Bhambra's way forward? Here I must encourage you to read the full argument for I can only summarize. She advocates a pluralism of voices, but is clear that allowing alternative voices alone is insufficient if that results merely in cacophony or a more subtle form of hegemonic tolerance. By contrast, relativism and enhanced boundary control lead merely to isolation from the mainstream. The different voices have, in short, to *connect* – to relate, to overlap, perhaps partially to converge, certainly to learn from each other in an open and respectful way. We should be grateful to her in starting us on this journey of mutual discovery.

Robin Cohen
University of Oxford

Preface and Acknowledgements

This book is an attempt to make good on questions raised by my father, questions that others with my social and cultural background may recognize from their own diasporic experiences. My father was a man who, enjoying the freedoms that independence from colonial rule brought, journeyed across India by train reading newspapers, consuming literature, talking to the peoples he encountered and arguing with them. Arguing, always arguing, against those who lamented the departure of the British, against those who expressed forms of dependency, whether intellectual or other, against those who saw the British Empire as a force for good in the world. Instead, he spoke to them about exploitation, about appropriation, about dispossession, and about the profound injustices and injuries of over two centuries of colonization. Much later he would question my own bland assertions drawn from a standard British schooling that drew attention to the horrors of Stalinism, but had nothing to say about the genocides of native peoples in the lands that came to be known as the Americas, as New Zealand, as Australia and as South Africa. He questioned the assertion that there was no democracy in countries such as Cuba by asking what I knew of the problems that any democracy might face that challenged Western hegemony. What did I know of the overthrow of the democratically elected Allende, of the murder of Lumumba, of countless other instances by way of which the Third World project was undermined? In his refusal to accept as truth the stated truths of the colonizer, he was the first to teach me to question, to ask 'is that really so?'

Writing this book has coincided with the systematic dismantling of public higher education in England where the very processes of knowledge production are also at stake. The mass, or public, university did not only open its doors to a more diverse demographic – that is, to women, the working-classes, black and minority ethnic people – but there was also an opening up of the curriculum and what (and whose) knowledge was validated. It is no accident that the government that is closing down the spaces for public higher education is also the government that wants the history curriculum for schools, for example, to be organized around a narrow interpretation of *Our Island Story*; a history book for children written by Henrietta Marshall in 1905 where British history was understood only in terms of the events that took place within the territorial bounds of the nation. What this misses, however, is that from its very inception as a nation, Britain has also been imperial and therefore its history has always been more extensive than the narrow parochialism now being promoted. How we represent the past is central to the politics of the present and it should be no surprise, then, that with the promotion of narrow and exclusive histories come narrow-minded policies in their wake – the 'Go Home' campaign in the summer of 2013 is one such example. Defending the public university is about defending the processes of democratization that have begun to open up knowledge production for all – knowledge is power, and if we don't reverse these current changes, we are facing a future in which power will, more explicitly, be knowledge.

This book is written in the hope that a more adequate address of our past within sociological considerations of the present will enable the opening up of different, and better, futures.

My deepest thanks go to those with whom I share the intellectual and political project to which this book is a contribution. While we have different responses and arguments, the questions we are seeking to explore provide a common ground for intellectual engagement and scholarship. For being part of this conversation and for all that you contribute to the making possible of other worlds, I would like to thank Ipek Demir, Peo Hansen, John Holmwood, Stefan Jonsson, Vicky Margree, Lucy Mayblin, John Narayan and Robbie Shilliam. I would also like to thank Vicky Margree and Robbie Shilliam for providing constructive comments on various chapters and Alice Mah and John Holmwood who provided excellent feedback across the whole book. John, in particular, read this manuscript many more times than any individual should have to and it is far better as a consequence of his engagement than it otherwise would have been.

This book has been 'in process' for a number of years and I thank, in particular, my publishers, Bloomsbury Academic, for their patience. Emily Drewe initially approached me with a request to write a book and somehow I found myself having agreed not only to write a book, but also to edit a series. Caroline Wintersgill took over from Emily and has been consistently supportive and immensely helpful across both my roles, as editor and author – I thank them both for their professionalism and collegiality. The University of Warwick has provided an intellectual home during the process of writing and I thank my colleagues in Sociology, History, Politics and Classics for their interdisciplinary commitments and scholarly engagements that have enabled the space for the articulation of the arguments made here. I would like to acknowledge the interactions, conversations and debates with the many Warwick students who have taken my modules on Global Historical Sociology, Global Sociology, Sociology and Postcolonialism, and Global Modernities, where various arguments made within the book were first tried out.

I have also presented these arguments at a number of confer-ences and seminars and I thank the organizers for the invitations that enabled me to discuss these issues with diverse audiences: Engin Isin, Deorientalizing Citizenship? Oecumene: Citizenship After Orientalism, Open University; Sandra Ponzanesi, Postcolonial Europe Network, Utrecht University; Rainer Forst, Philosophy and Social Science conference, Prague; Alf Nilsen, Bergen University; Esperança Bielsa, Symposium on Cosmopolitan Connections, Faculty of Philosophy, Universitat de Barcelona; Stefan Jonsson, Austere Histories of Europe Symposium, Linköping University, Norrköping; Zdenek Kavan, School of Global Studies, University of Sussex; Walter Mignolo and Rolando Vázquez, Decolonial summer school, Roosevelt Academy and Utrecht University; Wiebke Keim, International Conference on Circulating Social Science Knowledge, Institute of Sociology, University of Freiburg; Rodrigo Cordero, Faculty of Social Sciences and History,

Universidad Diego Portales, Santiago; Mauro di Meglio, University L'Orientale, Naples; Neera Chandhoke, Developing Countries Research Centre, University of Delhi. During 2013, I was a visiting academic, at the invitation of Gunlög Fur, at the Concurrences in Colonial and Postcolonial Studies Centre, Linnaeus University, Växjö and, at the invitation of Marcelo Rosa, at the Department of Sociology, University of Brasilia. I would like to thank them both for enabling me to spend time at their institutions and for the thoughtful and productive interactions with colleagues in both places.

Much as I see scholarship as a collective project and should like to share any responsibilities for errors and weaknesses the book might contain, they are, of course, my own.

frameworks based upon them. In deconstructing the histories of modernity that are placed at the core of the sociological endeavour, I hoped to open up space to think about sociology differently through an acknowledgement of other histories and experiences as well as to enable a reconsideration of the relations between disciplines. In this way, *Rethinking Modernity* pointed to the reconstruction that was necessary if we were to establish a sociology in the present that was different from the sociology of the past and, indeed, enable us to put that earlier sociology into the past.

Connected Sociologies seeks to deliver upon that call for reconstruction. It extends the earlier arguments to offer an alternative way forward, both in terms of the substance of what is recognized as sociology's past and a consideration of how this would alter the way in which we think about sociology in the present and the future. It points to the historical connections generated by processes of colonialism, enslavement, dispossession and appropriation, that were previously elided in mainstream sociology in favour of narrower understandings, as well as to the use of 'connections' as a way of recuperating these alternative histories, and, therefore, sociologies. If *Rethinking Modernity* addressed the parochial character of the histories at the heart of sociology's understanding of the emergence of the modern world, *Connected Sociologies* takes issue with the ways in which the global has come to be reconceptualized, across a variety of sociological traditions and perspectives, after a 'global turn' in the wake of a perceived recent phase of globalization. The past and its sociological forms of misrecognition, I argue, continue to constrain our ability to imagine different futures.

I

The perspective of 'connected sociologies', from which the book proceeds, starts from a recognition that events are constituted by processes that are always broader than the selections that bound events as particular and specific to their theoretical constructs. It is inspired by the call, by historian Sanjay Subrahmanyam (1997, 2005a, 2005b), for 'connected histories' which, he argues, do not derive from a singular standpoint, whether that be a putatively universal standpoint – which postcolonial theorists have demonstrated as being in fact a particular standpoint linked to colonialism – or a standpoint of the generalized subaltern. Indeed, both a particular standpoint and a universal standpoint in historical sociology tend to be strongly associated with a methodology of ideal types whose constructions are derived from particular value-relevant selections. Their disagreement is over the values deemed relevant, not over the form of the theoretical constructs to which they give rise. To understand events in terms of ideal types is to argue that they are knowable in terms of processes represented as internal to the type. Connected sociologies, in contrast, seek to reconstruct theoretical categories – their relations and objects – to create new understandings that incorporate and transform previous ones.

While knowledge can never be total, the selections we make have consequences for its ordering. That ordering is always open to challenge in the light of different selections and re-orderings. In the standard accounts of ideal types, the consequence is a plurality of processes that are disconnected precisely because the function of ideal types is to separate some events and 'entities' from others and to represent their internal relationships, thereby making other entities and events mere contingencies from the perspective of those relations. The approach of connected sociologies is different. It recognizes a plurality of possible interpretations and selections, not as a 'description', but as an opportunity for reconsidering what we previously thought we had known. Mere contingencies from one perspective become central features in another. This is not an argument for relativism (that is already implicit in standard ideal type methodology), but an argument for the reconstruction of concepts and the reinterpretation of histories in the light of that reconstruction.

The different sociologies in need of connection are themselves located in time and space, including the time and space of colonialism, empire and (post)colonialism. They will frequently arise as discordant and challenging voices and may even be resisted on that basis (a resistance made easier by the geo-spatial stratification of the academy). If some scholars experience their cherished sociological approaches to be under attack by new forms of particularism and localism, it is no response to assert a hegemonic particularism, now represented as 'our tradition'. The consequence of different perspectives must be to open up examination of events and processes such that they are understood differently in light of that engagement. Put another way, engaging with different voices must move us beyond simple pluralism to make a difference to what was initially thought; not so that we come to think the same, but that we think differently from how we had previously thought.

This is the push to reconstruction central to my conception of 'connected sociologies', whereby understandings are reconstructed as a consequence of the significant new connections identified. To put it most strongly, there is no connection where there is no reconstruction; and no understanding remains unchanged by connection. To understand events through their connections is to acknowledge from the outset that addressing particular sets of connections leads to particular understandings which are put in question through choosing other sets of connections. This is not a choice guided by whim, but through an argument for why certain connections were initially chosen and why choosing others could lead to more adequate explanations.

It is perhaps understandable that those challenging dominant positions are most clear about what they bring to the epistemological encounter, while those experiencing themselves under challenge often experience it only as loss of meaning and not the gain of an interlocutor. However, as has frequently been pointed out by postcolonial writers, those who encounter a hegemonic position are formed by it at the same time as they challenge it. What is unrecognized by those who are challenged is the asymmetry of recognition that this involves. So, while this is explicitly a book of critique, in the light of connected sociologies, it is nonetheless a work of sociological reconstruction formed by the positions it criticizes as well as by the critiques it mobilizes.

II

From its inception, classical sociology was less interested in the delineation of understandings of the global than in examining what were understood to be the European origins of global processes. Both Karl Marx (1976 [1867]) and Max Weber (1905), for example, sought to outline the peculiar conditions of Europe vis-à-vis the rest of the world that they believed to have given rise to the world-historical processes of capitalism (for discussion, see Bhambra 2011a). Indeed, as Eisenstadt puts it, the main issue of the comparative historical sociology that classical sociology inaugurated was to understand 'the peculiar "qualitative" and "descriptive" characteristics of pre-modern European and non-European societies in relation to, and especially in contrast with, modern (initially European) societies' (1974: 225). Classical sociologists, then, may have differed in significant aspects of their approaches, but they shared a common core emphasis on the European origins of capitalist modernity.

For Marx (1976 [1867]), capitalism was to be understood in terms of the specific changes in the 'local' social relations of small-scale production (so-called 'primitive accumulation') that contributed to the emergence of industrial societies in Western Europe, later to spread across the rest of the world. The same topic was approached by Weber (1905) through a comparative historical sociology of world religions that sought to identify a specifically European develo-pment, the Protestant Reformation, which gave rise to the 'spirit' of capitalism. This unique economic motivation, together with other favourable material conditions, was seen to have brought about the development of a capitalist world order. For both Marx and Weber, the global was something that came into being as a consequence of the diffusion of ideas and practices whose origins could be identified in Europe. Their starting point of what has been called 'European exceptionalism' led them to examine social and economic processes in other parts of the world in terms of their differences from Europe and as obstacles to the development of capitalism locally – for example, as in the Asiatic mode of production for Marx, or Chinese cultural constraints for Weber. Further, there was little to no consideration of how the already existing historical connections between parts of the world might be implicated in developments that were perceived as endogenous and independent processes exported to other parts of the world. Broader connections were discussed only as consequent to the future diffusion, spread and entanglement of the processes separately identified.

The 'global', insofar as it can be inferred from the writings of Marx and Weber, was the space in which processes initiated in Europe *came to play out as 'world-historical'*. There was little discussion of how the global might be understood in terms of processes not directly identified as *capitalist* but nonetheless contributing to modernity (for example, colonial settlement, dispossession, enslavement and other forms of appropriation). Their attention was, very firmly, on understanding developments of social relations within Europe, where the rest of the world served as a foil to such understandings, and working out the consequences *for* global others as they became 'world-historical'. The failure to recognize prior global connections, or to regard them as significant for capitalism, can be attributed, in part at least, to the elision of colonialism and empire to capitalism within their approaches. This was an elision that saw colonialism as not integral to the emergence and development of capitalist modernity, but as a distortion of it, similar, perhaps, to the obstacles identified with pre-capitalist modernity, while empire was barely addressed as a geopolitical form. The consequence of this for the classical tradition in sociology is that what needed to be explained were the particular conditions within Europe that had enabled its dominance upon the world. Once dominant, the rest of the world could simply be subsumed within Europe, or more properly, within European understandings which were thereby universalized.

Given the presumption of European exceptionalism and actual European dominance, it was held within classical sociology that, while there might be historically interesting societal and cultural variations, there was not anything to be learnt from the rest of the world, at least not contemporaneously. Slavery, for example, was allowed to appear as a significant topic in terms of its empirical manifestation in Atlantic societies, but it was not generally understood to be sociologically interesting from the perspective of the construction of the core categories of modernity. The leading post-classical theorist, Talcott Parsons (1966, 1971), for example, did not make any reference to slavery in his account of modern societies notwithstanding its role in the very society he deemed to be the new 'lead' society of modernity. Indeed, in common with social and political theorists who had lived contemporaneously with chattel slavery, slavery, when discussed conceptually, was an issue of pre-modern, 'ancient', societies not central to the emergence of modern ones. This is in contrast to the work of W. E. B. DuBois (1935) – and other largely unrecognized African American pioneers of US sociology such as Oliver Cromwell Cox and E. Franklin Frazier (see Saint-Arnaud (2009) – where chattel slavery is made central to the understanding of the modern US and to modernity more generally. The failure to acknowledge this tradition of scholarship as central to the self-understanding of sociology is a displacement both of the specifically African American contribution to sociology and of the processes of enslavement and colonization from modernity.[2]

Colonialism, then, had both created an effective global space and an elision of its continued role in the determination of social processes within that space. European hegemony, not being in question, would lead the way either to a global iron cage of modernization or, eventually, to contradiction, transformation and world Communism. Even if there

---

[2] A more thorough-going discussion of the implications and consequences of this displacement, for sociology in general, is given in Bhambra (2014).

was critique of specific colonial practices and sympathy for those subject to it, at least in the writings of Marx, there was nonetheless a justification of colonialism as hastening the development and spread of modern capitalism en route to the subsequent stage of world history and human emancipation. As a 'stages' theory of history was dominant, 'progress' was believed to be uni-directional and irreversible so the focus on Europe was further justified as it was to show the way for the rest of the world. While colonial expansion had constituted the global, it was not regarded by Marx or Weber as significant to the key relationships integral to the historical development of modern European societies or their subsequent (successful) trajectories. For example, while the expansion of the market was crucial to the development of capitalism and was driven along the tracks of colonial expansion, it was the relationships held to be intrinsic to the market that were the focus of attention, not the conditions under which it was expanded. With colonial expansion displaced from the construction of the core sociological accounts of modernity, it was also deemed to be of little relevance to the subsequent development of sociology. With modernity and modernization (whether capitalist or post-capitalist) as the only possibility, the rest of the world was to be drawn into the worlds created by Europe and Europeans and was to be understood in those terms.

III

The dominance of Europe, then, contributed to the invisibility of the global as subsumed under Europe, where Europe and modernity were one. Of course, the empirical reality of colonialism could not be denied despite its bland representation as resolved through processes of 'normal' development. The societies that were addressed via modernization theory were societies subject to colonial domination, even if that domination and resistance to it was not a major feature of sociological accounts. It was not until the global order constituted by colonialism visibly fractured that these other societies came into (European and North American) view in their own right. The convulsions in the early-to-mid twentieth century of the two world wars and, in particular, the emergence of the competing regimes of fascism (defeated) and Communism (resurgent), together with the movements of decolonization, dramatically reconfigured the world. The beginnings of a decline of western European hegemony and the shift in the landscape of the global, from being organized in colonial terms to being organized around (the desire for) nation states, necessitated developments within sociology in order to address the limitations of post-classical accounts of modernity (see Eisenstadt 1974).

Whereas previously an easy division had been made between modern, industrial societies and traditional, agrarian ones, this division was now perceived to be complicated for a number of reasons. In part, this was a consequence of traditional societies now being located within their own national states as opposed to within the ambit of broader colonial regimes (and the self-understandings of their implicit developmental teleologies). Given the similarity of political form, the nation state, this also blurred the boundaries between commonly accepted understandings of the traditional and modern. National elites within traditional societies, for example, were commonly seen as 'modernizing elites' and so new problems related to the relationship between modern states, modernizing elites and traditional societies (masses) were posed for the social sciences. Further, the explicit ideological break among what were understood as modern societies that became embodied in the Cold War division between the Communist Soviet Union and the capitalist United States meant that there was no longer simply one acknowledged route to modernization. Modernizing elites, in what came to be called the Third World, were faced with a choice of pre-established routes. Or they could choose to articulate their own visions for development as many of the countries signing up to the Non-Aligned Movement sought to do (see Prashad 2007). Decolonization and the establishment of independent nation states had not only brought the unevenness of development across the globe into sharp relief, but also pointed to the different routes to modernity that might be available to 'traditional' societies.

Modernization theory was one attempt to address these issues, but, given the political situation, it was closely followed by underdevelopment and dependency theory reflecting a more critical approach to alternatives. This was so, not simply within the Western academy but also in terms of the emergence of theorists of decolonization and then postcolonialism located in, and addressing, a variety of other contexts. Even if 'currently existing' Communism was identified by few scholars as the true alternative to capitalism that Marx had envisaged, its very presence as an alternative created the space for thinking of different alternatives. It also acted as a 'goad' to liberal democracies in terms of indicating the necessity of addressing issues of inequality, including racial inequality, exclusion and civil rights. As Dudziak argues, in the context of the US, the international focus on racial segregation and the political, social and economic subordination of African Americans contradicted the espousal of American democracy as enlightened and egalitarian – that is, as modern – and hampered 'their ability to sell [their version of] democracy to the Third World' (1988: 62–3). Notwithstanding any limitations attributed to modernization theory's view of convergence as a process of modernity, then, convergence did at least also imply the further modification of the societies associated with the exemplary form. In this way, not only was modernity understood to be differentiated, but its 'exemplary' form was regarded as unfinished and, in principle, reformable. The meaning of modernity was at stake and 'Eurocentric'[3] accounts did not seem to hold all the cards.

From the perspective of developments in mainstream sociological theory, however, this critical moment in approaches to the idea

---

[3] In this book, the term 'Eurocentric' refers generally to the understandings of the global north and its southern 'outposts'. For example, the dominant understandings of North America are continuous with those of the Europe from which it claims a substantial part of its heritage and for whom North America was part of its imaginary. Of course, Europe as a geopolitical entity is diverse, but the idea of Eurocentrism is associated with a particular way of representing a unifying set of characteristics across that diversity; a set of characteristics that even those proclaiming the diverse histories of Europe nonetheless generally sign up to as the framework within which diversity is expressed.

of the 'global' – a moment when dominant Western ideas were under challenge – passed. The collapse of Communism in Europe in the late 1980s dramatically altered the context for sociological self-understandings of the discipline and its worlds. With the absorption of Communist Europe to its 'other', the moment of alternatives, of non-alignment, and even of reform was ostensibly over.[4] This moment both heralded a new phase in sociological theory oriented to a future of globalization, notwithstanding the globalized nature of what preceded it, and a consciousness of the limitations of current sociological theory. These limitations were associated primarily with critiques of modernization theory, but the proposed sociological reconstruction – 'multiple modernities' – came to look very much like modernization theory rebooted. As I shall argue, theorists of multiple modernities associate all positive normative substance to the European idea of modernity where the multiple other possibilities of (mostly non-European) modernity are seen to be largely authoritarian in nature and, unlike the European idea, not universalizable.

With multiple modernities, the authoritarian nature of 'European modernity' itself, deriving from its colonial origins, is once again displaced. The critiques by theorists of decolonization and postcolonialism are dismissed as having no real purchase on contemporary issues in light of the new sociological reformulations. To the extent that any significance is attributed to them, it is in terms of acknowledging the limitations of previous sociological understandings, but without contributing in any way to the critical substance of those reformulations. As such, in arguing for the continued significance of postcolonial histories and critique, both in their own terms and in terms of how these histories continue to structure the present, I am not posing an alternative modernity outside a trajectory common to the West; rather,

---

4   To take the US context again, the commitment of the government to achieve racial equality, as Dudziak presciently noted, is 'diminished by the degree to which Cold War motives were satisfied' (1988: 119). More recent scholarship confirms this view (King and Smith 2011).

I am arguing for a reconstructed understanding of modernity inclusive of its colonial histories and their consequences.

What is also absent from the account of multiple modernities is any address of the change in the nature of the form it holds to be exemplary and the implications of this for the standard normative understandings of modernity. Whereas earlier modernization theorists had argued for a *reformed and reformable* modernity, theorists of multiple modernities, who otherwise stress endogenous processes, have little to say about the internal processes giving rise to widening inequality and the dismantling of the achievements that the previous generation associated with modernity. Further, a reduction of the 'social' to the economic – the neo-liberal global project, for example – is seen to be the product of processes of globalization external to Europe and no longer the process Europe inaugurated. As we shall see when considering Beck's arguments about cosmopolitanism in a later chapter, any negative change in the normative content of modernity is associated with external processes, whereas all positive content derives from endogenous European processes.

IV

The previous section has set out the broad context for the book, though, of course, the specifics of the different theories are more complex. The purpose of the book is to get behind these complexities in order to understand the deeper structures of thinking that characterize the hegemonic sociological account of modernity despite its appearance of variety.

The first section of *Connected Sociologies* addresses the way in which ideas of the global have figured within two dominant modes of sociology: theoretical and historical. It addresses the former in terms of the approaches of modernization theory, underdevelopment and dependency theory, and multiple modernities, and the latter through a focus on Marxist and Weberian forms of historical sociology. The idea of the global, within the first chapter, is understood in theoretical terms, that is, it is given definition by the frameworks of the approaches under consideration. Modernization theory, for example, effectively understood the global as a contested space within which not-yet-modern countries were faced with the choice of modernizing along the lines of the United States or the Soviet Union. So, in this sense, the global was an empty space to be populated and defined according to the ideological commitments of newly modernizing countries. This is contrasted with underdevelopment and dependency theories which saw the global as the uneven terrain created as a consequence of the processes of capitalism and to be accounted for in these terms. While these modes of thought were dominant within mainstream sociology in the 1960s and 1970s, they fell out of favour by the 1980s and, after the collapse of Communism within Europe, were largely replaced by the approach of multiple modernities. Within this approach, under-standings of the global were framed through a theoretical commitment to civilizational analysis.

The second chapter, in contrast, looks at the way in which the idea of the global has been articulated within sociology through a direct address of the historical record by writers concerned with the 'formalism' of modernization theory. This chapter examines the work of Fernand Braudel, a historian with social-scientific sympathies, and of two historical-sociologists, the Weberian Michael Mann and the Marxist Immanuel Wallerstein. It examines their respective projects of writing a world history (as opposed to a history of the world), of delin-eating the sources of social power, and articulating an understanding of the emergence of world systems. All three seek to develop an under-standing of the global and global processes through a consideration of historical sources and this chapter discusses the extent to which their 'world-histories' or 'world-historical-sociologies' are cognizant of the worlds of which they speak. While the first two chapters focus on attempts by sociologists either to articulate a theoretical framework within which the global could be understood, or to delineate a historically informed understanding of the global, the second section addresses work by sociologists who seek to rethink sociology in light of a more recent 'global turn'.

The calls by Immanuel Wallerstein and colleagues to 'open the social sciences' and by Ulrich Beck for a cosmopolitan social science are the focus of the third chapter. Both start from the position that recent transformations in the world are necessitating radical transformations of the ways in which we examine and seek to understand that world. There is general agreement that the social sciences emerged in the nineteenth century to address the problems and challenges associated with the newly formed nation states. While the social sciences were seen to be adequate in those terms, and times, it is suggested that with the shift to the global and the potential dissolution of nation states, the social sciences themselves need to be transformed. The difference between Wallerstein and Beck is that while Beck regards the social sciences to have been appropriate for their time, that is, the nineteenth century, Wallerstein wishes to argue for a more substantial transformation. The focus of Wallerstein and Beck is on the necessary transformation of the social sciences in the context of globalization, but, I suggest, they remain tied to specific European genealogies.

The following two chapters look at other calls for 'global sociology' made from various locations around the globe and in relation to traditions of social thought other than those usually associated with Europe and the West. The first of these, Chapter 4, looks at the development of a specifically global sociology as argued for by scholars associated with the International Sociological Association. The Association, both through its meetings and its journals, provides an important space for the articulation and wider dissemination of ideas of 'global sociology' from scholars based in geographically plural locations. This chapter addresses the contributions of Akinsola Akiwowo in arguing for a re-examination of the relationship between indigenization and the internationalization of sociology. It is followed by a discussion of arguments around dependency and subversion made in the Latin American context and also addresses calls for the development of autonomous social science traditions as argued for by Syed Farid Alatas and others. Chapter 5 continues this discussion by looking at related arguments for Southern theory and against Northern epistemologies as articulated by Raewyn Connell and Boaventura de Sousa Santos respectively. It also addresses the work of Sujata Patel and Michael Burawoy, who have been actively promoting ideas of global sociology and arguing for a 'provincialized' or subaltern social science through the International Sociological Association and other such venues. These chapters close the specific engagement, on the one hand, with sociological understandings of the global and, on the other, with the way in which sociology is itself shaped by its particular understanding of the global.

The argument of the book, across the first two sections, examines the insufficiencies and limitations of standard sociological understandings of the global from a variety of perspectives. The final two chapters present a possible alternative to the standard accounts, drawing upon the traditions of postcolonial and decolonial thought. The penultimate chapter establishes the resources provided by these traditions for both a different historical understanding of the global and a different mode of understanding the global. The implications of this for sociology are established in the final chapter further articulating the epistemological and methodological contours of 'connected sociologies'.

The point I shall be making throughout is not simply that there is a series of alternative histories to be acknowledged, but that in doing so, what is involved is a reformed understanding of the processes represented within dominant histories. To the extent that the latter reinforce particular sets of concepts as central to the understanding of modernity, this will also involve a displacement and reformulation of those concepts. 'Connected sociologies', I suggest, are not simply artic- ulations of different narratives, but are the means of understanding sociology and its tasks differently, an endeavour which is pressing in the light of the global issues that confront us.

Part One

Sociological Theory and Historical Sociology

1

Modernization Theory, Underdevelopment and Multiple Modernities

Notwithstanding Marx's hopes for a post-capitalist future, both he and Weber could be said to share a pessimism about capitalist modernity. For Weber, it was an 'iron cage', while for Marx, in the absence of radical transformation, it involved the reproduction of exploitation and class domination. This pessimism was replaced in post-war US scholarship by a strong belief in the possibilities, as opposed to inherent limitations, of industrial capitalist society. As Jeffrey Alexander suggests, the present was no longer viewed 'as a way station to an alternative social order, but, rather, as more or less the only possible system there ever could be' (1995: 16). However, it had proven to be reformable in ways not imagined by Weber. This was not to suggest that there were no contemporary alternatives, but rather that post-war US society represented, to (mostly, white) US sociologists, the pinnacle of human achievement – a modern, democratic, industrial capitalist society which appeared to guarantee economic growth and prosperity for (most of) its citizens. It was a system that had contributed to the defeat of fascism in Europe and, in the process, had replaced a war-weakened Europe as the 'lead society' of modernization, as suggested by Talcott Parsons (1971) among many others. At the same time, however, it was confronted for dominance on the world stage, by the simultaneous rise of the Soviet Union, which had also contributed to the defeat of fascism in Europe. It similarly sought to guarantee economic growth and decent living standards for its citizens, but this time organized around a political programme of industrial Communism.

The Cold War hostilities between the US and the Soviet Union were manifest also in the development of academic theories to account for their similarities and differences. It could not be denied that the Soviet Union had modernized on a par with the US and now presented countries, which were believed to be in the process of modernization, with an alternative to the path taken by the US. In the dominant US literature, Soviet modernization was presented as a deviant form that came about as a consequence of 'a disease of the transition', where the disease was identified as Communism and state intervention (Rostow 1960: 163). Nonetheless, it was seen to be potentially appealing to those 'aspiring societies of the world', who were yet to modernize, and scholars such as Rostow urged the US and the West more generally to 'mobilise their ample resources to do the jobs that must be done' to ensure the victory of the 'democratic north' (1960: 164, 104–5, 167). To this end, modernization theory developed as a way of presenting the elements of reform-oriented modernization within democratic Western countries and, therefore, providing a model of the 'correct' way to modernize for other countries. In this chapter, I will set out the key features of this model, its critique in underdevelopment and dependency theory, before addressing the revival of modernization theory in accounts of multiple modernities (albeit with the orientation to reform and amelioration considerably muted).

I

Drawing on the experience of Western modernization, scholars such as Lerner (1958), Levy (1965) and Rostow (1960) sketched out a model of modernization that they believed ought to have global applicability. At the conceptual level, Levy argued that the patterns of relatively modernized societies demonstrated a universal tendency to affect all other social contexts 'whose participants have come in contact with them' (1965: 30). In the process, he continued, 'the previous indigenous patterns always change; and they always change in the direction of the some of the patterns of the relatively modernized society' (1965: 30). Substantively, the sorts of elements of modernized society under discussion included the processes of rural–urban migration, growing population density, increasing literacy, mass media, free markets and the organization of democratic political participation (Lerner 1958). The model developed from an examination of modernized (Western) countries was then used to study other societies and determine the extent of their approximation to (Western) modernization. It could also be used, as Shah (2011) suggests, to provide the information needed by the US to intervene more effectively in those countries it deemed to be at risk of succumbing to Soviet influence. Beyond its contribution to geopolitics, however, modernization theory also, more generally, normalized a particular trajectory of development and established a global frame within which all societies could be placed.

While modernization theory was presented as a conceptual framework against which empirical investigations of countries could be compared and assessed, a regular feature was the similarity of Western processes with the framework and the deviation of other countries from it. Almond and Coleman's (1960) classic study, for example, examines the politics of developing areas and discusses the extent to which the countries under comparison align with or deviate from the conceptual framework. In their conclusion, they discuss the possibilities of different routes to modernization and distinguish between 'normal' forms influenced by 'ideals of democracy, equality, and the social welfare state' and 'deviant' ones influenced by 'the modernizing authoritarianism of Ataturk or of Soviet Communism' (1960: 552). As Bernstein (1971) commented, it was hardly surprising that, within the framework of this model, Western countries most closely approximated it. After all, the model was itself derived from a study of Western experience.

Almond and Coleman (1960) recognize, in general terms, the impact of modern European colonialism in determining the different political systems of developing countries. However, they have very little to say on colonization as such and the way in which it has historically had an impact upon the possibilities *for* development. Moreover, there is no recognition of postcolonial effects with consequences beyond the immediate presence of a colonial power. For example, their classificatory scheme allows for a category of 'terminal colonial democracy', a form that terminates precisely with independence. Even where racial segregation as a consequence of colonialism is acknowledged, as in South Africa or Southern Rhodesia (when they were writing), the 'European' institutions are those of 'an essentially modern political system' (1960: 574) and are not themselves deformed by their colonial constitution. In contrast to other forms of authoritarianism, such as fascism and Bolshevism, colonialism, then, is presented in largely neutral terms.

The absence of a proper address of the consequences of colonialism within the modernization paradigm is evident also in the failure to address the structures of racism consequent to enslavement and segregation that constitute the modern society of the US against which the developing areas are being assessed.[1] This had consequences not only for the way in which 'underdevelopment' was understood, but also for the representation of the US itself, the society regarded as the lead society of modernization. As I have already commented, the issue of racial inequality was increasingly seen as significant in terms of the perception of US democracy abroad. For example, in his Introduction to *The Negro American* – a book edited with Kenneth Clark and with a Foreword by the then President Lyndon B. Johnson – Talcott Parsons wrote of 'the world-wide symbolic significance of the American color problem' (1967: xxiii). Beyond the symbolic significance, however, there was also an unacknowledged epistemological significance.[2]

[1] This, despite the extensive scholarship by, mostly African American, social scientists addressing the implications of 'the peculiar institution' within modern US politics and society (see, for example, DuBois 1935; Myrdal 1944; Ellison 1973 [1944]; Frazier 1947; Cox 1970 [1948]; Parsons and Clark 1967).

[2] This is also evident when Parsons returns to the issues in his 'theory of the societal community' left uncompleted at his death in 1979 and finally published in 2007 as *American Society*. The issues of ethnicity are issues of '*Gemeinschaft*', that is, social integration and the symbolic realm not structural features of the political and economic

While authoritarianism is perceived as a form of 'pathological' modernity and measured against the 'normal' form of Western modernity, colonialism and enslavement as forms of authoritarianism intrinsic to that 'normal' form are not addressed. Parsons concurred with his co-editor Kenneth Clark in his argument that 'the very definition of a *category* of citizens as inherently inferior is an anomaly ... basically incompatible with our social principles and organization' (1967: xxv). He further argued that the type of modern society that 'we have been developing has for *both* moral and structural reasons *no* legitimate place for such a category' (1967: xxv). If racial inequality had no structural 'legitimacy', however, the problem was to understand how it had a structural place. Segregation and discrimination were structural features of US society and this society was to be interpreted through a theory of modernization which was intended to provide the means of structural analysis. It is significant to note that the 20-year anniversary of Myrdal's (1944) *An American Dilemma* was the occasion of the edited collection, and yet this was the first time that Parsons had addressed the topic of race. Moreover, this late address of race coincided with his writing of *Societies: Evolutionary and Comparative Perspectives* (1966) and *The System of Modern Societies* (1971), neither of which sought to address the structural lacunae that Parsons implicitly acknowledged (with no references to race or chattel slavery in either volume and thus no consideration of their structural relationship to modernity). Apparently, the 'normal' processes of modernity would eliminate a problem that was nonetheless coterminous with modernity and unexplained in its categories.

Within modernization theory, the contemporary global was understood empirically as a contested space in which the newly decolonized

system. He notes a shift in usage from 'Negro' to 'Black' and increasing references to 'Afro-Americans', which he believes creates a parallel and symmetry both with other ethnically identified groups – such as Chinese and Japanese Americans – but also with what he calls the 'indigenous American white population' (2007: 327). As should be clear, this elides the very processes by which a population is represented as indigenous and also the different processes associated with experiences of forced and voluntary migration.

countries had a choice, as they saw it, between following the model provided by the US or that provided by the Soviet Union. So while modernization theory recognized the global empirically as the site of different experiences and processes, it advocated a model which would involve all countries converging to its established framework. Differences that remained were identified in terms of variance from the model and were regarded as deviant or as demonstrating a failure of transition. Differences were not deemed to be significant in their own terms. In the same way, connections between countries and broader processes were recognized, but there was an attempt to subsume these connections to a model that was deemed to have global applicability; that is, while connections were recognized as empirically significant, they were not deemed to have any explanatory value – the model substituted for explanation. The model ultimately served to organize endogenous explanations of varieties of development and instituted a common linear teleology across those different, autonomous traditions and trajectories – a teleology to which all were, eventually, to converge. In this way, while modernization theory sought to engage with the social and political realities of other parts of the world, it did so by subsuming what was learnt to a pre-existing framework. As Tipps astutely identifies, '[f]ar from being a universally applicable schema for the study of the historical development of human societies, the nature of modernization theory reflects a particular phase in the development of a single society, that of the United States' (1973: 211).

Critiques of modernization theory were prevalent at the time both within US sociology, such as in the work of Henry Bernstein (1971), Dean Tipps (1973) and Alejandro Portes (1976), and in the emerging field of development studies. These critiques were oriented around the following themes. First, there was disquiet at 'the self-confidence of ethnocentric achievement', that was perceived to be a legacy of 'earlier notions of social evolution and Darwinism', and was at the heart of modernization theory (Mazrui 1968: 82). The belief was not simply that the West had achieved modernity, but that the move from tradition to modernity was a universal imperative and all societies would (eventually) undergo this transition. As a consequence, the universalization of what were understood to be Western values and institutions was accompanied by a relative disregard of the 'not-yet' modern societies under consideration; they were, after all, in the process of being superseded. Within modernization theory, then, these 'relatively modernizing' societies simply provided data which were to be 'gathered, sorted, and interpreted' against the stable categories and conceptual frameworks derived from the Western experience (Tipps 1973: 207). Alongside the normative critiques of modernization theory's ethnocentrism, there was also concern about the empirical validity of its categories.

The critiques of modernization theory rested on its problematic separation of tradition from the modern, its understanding of tradition as simply being that which was not modern, and its failure to address the impact of external factors in processes of modernization. As a number of anthropologists, for example, pointed out, the presentation of tradition within modernization theory was often as a 'hypothetical antithesis to "modernity"' and rarely rested upon empirical research (Tipps 1973: 212). Traditional societies were posited as stagnant, static, unchanging entities that required intervention to enable them to undertake an effective transition to modernity. As Wolf argues, by equating such societies with a lack of development, modernization theory denied them any significant history and 'blocked effective understanding of relationships among them' (1997 [1982]: 13). It failed to acknowledge that these societies had histories prior to European contact, had varieties of social formations that could not simply be lumped en masse under the heading 'traditional' and that European engagement through 'war, conquest, and colonial domination' (Tipps 1973: 212) needed to be taken into account in any attempt to address the nature and forms of social and political change within those countries. This latter point was one that was picked up by theorists who preferred to work with the terms development, underdevelopment or dependency instead of modernization. In doing this, they sought to address the limitations of modernization theory by looking explicitly at the way in which the emergence of capitalism had enabled development in the West at the same time as creating 'underdevelopment' and 'dependency' in the previously colonized countries and what were seen as 'weaker' nations.

II

Standard development studies correlated well with modernization theory given the similarity of their concerns with social progress and the possibilities of policy intervention to facilitate such processes. In this context, development was generally understood as a process, whereas underdevelopment, as Bernstein argues, was often 'conceived only in a static fashion as a *state*' (1976: 25) to be overcome by development. This naturalized the idea of underdevelopment as the inherent condition of traditional societies and inhibited the analysis of underdevelopment as a condition that had been actively *produced* in those countries. Underdevelopment theory and dependency theory emerged as ways of contesting such representations of traditional societies within standard sociological explanations of the processes of social change. In particular, these theories sought to link development to the emergence of capitalism and, in the process, to link underdevelopment and dependency to these same processes. As Leys succinctly outlines, the conditions prevailing within, what are regarded as 'underdeveloped' or 'less developed' countries, 'are not due to the persistence of an "original" (*un*developed or "untouched") state of affairs, but are the results of the same world-historical process in which the "First World" ("developed market economies") became "developed"' (1977: 92; see also Frank 1970). This world-historical process, in most accounts, was identified as 'capital seeking profits' (Leys 1977: 92). In this way, the international economy was seen to be a more productive starting point for understanding development and underdevelopment than any of the dominant, internalist concepts of standard sociology.[3] It was also an approach that, instead of blaming the countries that failed to conform to the expected model (and being labelled as deviant or pathological), looked to reconstruct theories and models on the basis of empirical evidence and historical analysis (Bernstein 1976: 22). In so doing, pathologies internal to standard accounts of modernity itself were also identified.

Dependency theory was a particular formulation within these broader debates initially articulated by a group of Latin American sociologists, including Fernando Cardoso (1972), Aníbal Quijano (1971) and Theotonio Dos Santos (1970), and popularized in the Western academy by their colleague and fellow protagonist, Andre Gunder Frank (1970). The field was constructed through a mutual engagement with the question of 'the development of Latin American capitalism' and offered a variety of explanations for the particular situation of Latin American countries with respect to 'the capitalism of the centre' (Palma 1978: 898). The common element between the approaches gathered under the '*dependentista*' rubric was, according to Palma, their concern 'to analyse Latin American societies through a "comprehensive social science", which stresses the socio-political nature of the economic relations of production' (1978: 911). This meant that development and underdevelopment were understood, not as autonomous, separate stages mapping onto the modern-tradition dualism of modernization theory, but as structurally interrelated and co-produced by the emergence and spread of capitalism across the world. As Dos Santos argued, dependence is 'a situation in which the economy of certain countries is conditioned by the development and expansion of another economy to which the former is subjected' and which enables us 'to see the internal situation of these countries as part of world economy' (1970: 231). Similarly, the rapid industrial growth of the West was to be understood in terms of 'the conditioning

---

[3] The latter is something that subsequently came to be described as methodological nationalism (see Chernilo 2007; Fine 2007), although, once again, it is worth noting that those making that accusation do not do so to draw attention to colonialism and empire.

of a "periphery" from which an economic surplus is extracted and necessary raw materials secured' (Portes 1976: 74; Wallerstein 1974a).

The introduction of the concept of 'dependence' helped to illuminate particular aspects of the broader debate, but also raised a number of additional problems. It was positive and productive in the sense of recognizing underdevelopment not as a stage of 'backwardness' or tradition, but rather as intrinsic to capitalist modernity and 'a necessary consequence of its evolution' (Portes 1976: 74). It also pointed to the necessity of examining the specificities of relationships between international corporations and the nature of their engagement with underdeveloped countries. On the downside, Lall, for example, suggested that dependence, as a descriptive category, said little about the nature of the economy as a whole or the condition of economic processes; and, as an analytic category, it was impossible to define. This was because, as he argued, 'in terms of static characteristics it is analytically impossible to draw a clear line between dependent and non-dependent economies', and in terms of the dynamics of dependence there was little agreement on what these might be (1975: 807). Lall therefore questioned the utility of bringing together all 'different types and stages of the capitalist development process ... under *one* category of dependence' (1975: 806). Being less developed could not be regarded as directly equivalent to being dependent. While 'dependence' was a useful corrective, pointing to the importance of relationships between societies deemed to be developed or underdeveloped, it, in turn, was believed to have subsumed all analysis to the meta-theoretical framework of capitalism. In this way, it seemed to deny the importance of local conditions or histories which might also provide useful resources for analysing differences between national societies.

As has been discussed, capitalism, or the international capitalist system, predominated as the frame of reference for the explanation of development, underdevelopment and dependency. While there was occasional mention of colonialism in this context, this was often in terms of Lenin's theory of imperialism (as a derived consequence of capitalist development) and debates related to that, rather than the historical existence and significance of colonial relations (see Alavi 1964; Hobson 1954 [1902]). Even where theorists such as Samir Amin (1973 [1971]) explicitly addressed the broader historical context of colonialism, the present economic situation and its ideological interpretation was, nonetheless, paramount in his analyses. His attention was more focused on the organization of economic relations in the capitalist system, and the possibilities for socialism, even as he addressed the histories that facilitated (or obstructed) these. Much of Amin's (1973 [1971]) early work, for example, addressed the implications of colonial exploitation for the creation of economic underdevelopment in West Africa. He examined the history of economic relations instituted by colonial powers to assess the ways in which parts of Africa were transformed from being 'virtually outside the world market, into that of a true underdeveloped economy: dominated by and integrated into the world market' (1973: xiv). The work was one of political economy, structured around the historical stages of colonial and then capitalist development, in order to understand present economic structures.

While Amin was one of the few initially to take a longer view, in the main, as Lall argues, the concept of dependence was 'essentially directed at the postcolonial era when direct forms of colonial subjugation had ended and new forms of "imperialism", which ensure dependence rather than open domination, had supervened' (1975: 800). Underdevelopment and dependency theorists were largely writing in the context of the emergence of newly decolonized nation states where the political domination of colonial powers had been overcome, but particular institutions, especially those associated with the economy, remained firmly in place. The concern here was to distinguish contemporary dependency from historical colonialism and to identify the economic structures and processes that enabled new forms of old patterns of domination to continue. In the Latin American context, dependency theory was further developed as a critique of the national bourgeoisie which was seen to be accumulating wealth for itself while impoverishing the rest of the population and came about in the wake of the success of the Cuban Revolution as demonstrating an alternative (non-capitalist) path of development (Grosfoguel 2000). In this context, the urgent need was for new economic policies that met the needs of the new inclusive political communities. For this reason, the radical variants of development studies were largely articulated by left-wing economists and Marxist sociologists.[4]

Many of the debates centred on particular interpretations of Marxism and on identifying the ways in which lesser developed countries were understood to be inserted into the international capitalist system and the ways in which they could find (possibly autonomous) routes to socialism. For some scholars, lesser developed countries had to become fully developed capitalist countries, fully integrated in the world capitalist system, before they could move to socialism; for others, there was the possibility of socialism via autonomous national development. Others further identified under-development not as a consequence of being invaded by foreign capital, but of being starved of it (Emmanuel 1974). As Booth suggests, by the 1980s, the development debate had reached an impasse with the majority of exchanges being 'between different poles of opinion within Marxism' (1985: 773). Instead of rigorous empirical work designed to understand how and why economic structures and processes worked in particular ways, Booth (1985) argues that much work in this area was more committed to demonstrating the necessity of those struc-tures to capitalism than to understanding them in their own terms. Further, while underdevelopment theory had emerged 'as *a criticism of bourgeois development theory*', it had nonetheless remained within its dominant theoretical framework (of addressing the 'problem' of underdevelopment and/or dependence) and this limited the extent to which it could offer a truly radical alternative (Leys 1977: 94). There

---

[4] The sensibilities of the economists were somewhat different from those now charac-teristic of the profession whereby concern with the practical problems of real world economies, especially those outside the West, has been displaced by the subsequent codification of a professional orthodoxy around neoclassical axioms (see Fourcade 2009; Yonay 1998; for discussion, see Holmwood 2013).

was a sense, as Leys argues, that the real gains of the work being done in this area, that is, 'the detailed analyses of the institutions and structures of underdevelopment' were 'being appropriated more by the ideologists of international capital than the workers and peasants of the Third World' (1977: 96).

An alternative came in the work of scholars such as Walter Rodney (1972) and Frantz Fanon (1963). While they were also provoked to write as a consequence of being concerned with the contemporary economic situation in Africa, their analyses of the historical emergence of underdevelopment and dependency were underpinned by broader social and political commitments. Both Fanon (1963) and Rodney (1972) articulated, much more forcefully than Amin and others, the idea of colonialism as the central aspect in the creation and maintenance of underdevelopment in Africa (and elsewhere) and, at the same time, as integral to the emergence and development of capitalism in Europe and the US. Fanon, for example, argued that the opulence of Europe 'has been founded on slavery, it has been nourished with the blood of slaves and it comes directly from the soil and from the subsoil of that underdeveloped world' (1963: 96). Similarly, Rodney extensively detailed the ways in which colonialism was not simply a system of exploitation, but was one which also appropriated and repatriated to the 'mother-country' the profits generated through the 'surplus produced by African labour out of African resources' (1972: 162). Both scholars further explicitly argued for the necessity of revolutionary struggle against colonial domination, as well as capitalism, as the way out of the current situation of dependency and underdevelopment. They were writing not so much to participate in the scholarly debates around the best ways forward for development studies or the correctness of any particular position within the Marxist debates on the international capitalist system, but rather, as Babu (1972) writes in the postscript to Rodney's *How Europe Underdeveloped Africa*, to arouse mass action by the people. Fanon and Rodney were exceptional in their time in their address of the colonial histories of recently decolonized and decolonizing countries in the wider debates on development and underdevelopment. Their continuing influence on scholars within the traditions of postcolonialism and decoloniality will be discussed subsequently.

The impasse within the scholarly debates on development, under-development and dependency was resolved in two quite different ways. One was an attempt to retain the Marxist frame through the articulation of a world systems theory that now saw dependence simply as an attribute of a particular historical and geographical period (which will be addressed in the following chapter); and the other was a rehabilitation of Weberian modernization theory through the paradigm of multiple modernities. If modernization theory reflected the post-war optimism and influence of the US upon the world stage, and under-development theory reflected the debates and struggles of those in the process of decolonization and establishing new nations, then the re-emergence of modernization theory in the 1990s was strongly correlated to the unexpected fall of Communism in Europe, which seemed to confirm some of the expectations of modernization theory that had been challenged by dependency theorists. It is to this latter development that this chapter now turns.

III

The ambition for the creation of a single world market after the break-up of the Soviet-dominated economic bloc erased the Cold War bipolarity that had existed both politically and in theoretical discussions concerning the best way forward in 'bourgeois' development studies and its radical alternatives in underdevelopment and dependency theories. The many critiques of modernization theory could not simply be ignored, but it was believed that the West had 'won' and that the success of liberal capitalist democracy signalled a possible 'end of history'. As Fukuyama noted, the majority of countries that had 'succeeded in achieving a high level of economic development have in fact come to look increasingly similar, rather than less' (1992: 133). While countries could take a variety of routes 'to get to the end of history,' he suggested that 'there are few versions of modernity other than the capitalist liberal-democratic one that look like they are going concerns' (1992: 133). This reaffirmation of modernization theory, however, was not completely uncritical. Fukuyama argued that the economic focus of modernization theory was limited and needed to be supplemented with an explicitly cultural argument about the desirability of modernity and 'the struggle for recognition as a major driver of history' (1992: 205). While there had previously been a viable alternative model of political and economic organization, as embodied in the Soviet Union, there was now believed to be a growing consensus around the claims of liberal capitalist democracy as the only rational and desirable model of governance. Even for Fukuyama, however, the question emerged that, if this was the case, then why was it just a universal *model*, and not universally in *existence* across all societies in the world.

It was in the attempt to explain both the seeming triumph of liberal capitalism and the continuing diversity and heterogeneity of existing societies that led to the reformulation of modernization theory as multiple modernities. Key to this reformulation was Shmuel Eisenstadt (1974, 2000a), earlier one of the main theorists of modernization, together with a core group of European historical-sociologists such as Arnason (2000, 2003) and Wittrock (1998), as well as critical interlocutors such as Göle (2000), Dirlik (2003) and Kaya (2004).[5]

In developing this new paradigm, it was believed that two main fallacies needed to be addressed. The first, in relation to modernization theory, was that there was only one form of modernization, one that approximated the experience of the West. The second, in relation to

---

[5] See the two special issues of *Daedalus*: 'Early Modernities', *Daedalus* 127 (1998) and 'Multiple Modernities', *Daedalus* 129 (2000). For further details on the sociological debates on modernization and the shift to multiple modernities, see Chapter 3 of my *Rethinking Modernity: Postcolonialism and the Sociological Imagination* (Bhambra 2000).

critiques made by theorists of underdevelopment and dependency, that looking from the West to the East was not necessarily a form of Orientalism or Eurocentrism. While it was accepted that the particular historical trajectories of societies beyond the West needed to be taken into consideration in discussing developments within modernity, modernity was nonetheless believed to be a European phenomenon in its origins. Therefore, the developing modernities of other places could be compared to the dominant form of European modernity, but there was no expectation that these other modernities would converge with the patterns of Europe. The focus here was on the acceptability of divergent paths and of the diversity of modern societies. This acceptance of diversity was believed to inoculate multiple modernities against charges of ethnocentrism or the inappropriate privileging of particular histories over other ones. The challenge faced by the multiple modernities paradigm was to acknowledge the diversity of types of modernity, without falling into a form of relativism, at the same time as arguing for liberal European modernity as the dominant version, without suggesting a form of triumphalism. I suggest it fails on both counts.

The key innovation made by theorists of multiple modernities was to include, as Fukuyama had before them, a cultural dimension to the standard economic understandings of modernization (although this failing could hardly be directed at most sociologists of modern-ization). They argued that modernity needed to be understood in terms of its institutional constellations, as embodied in the market and polity, as well as in its cultural configurations, that is, in its values and its orientations to autonomy and domination, and so forth. By splitting understandings of modernity in this way, theorists were able to argue for an institutional commonality (of state and market), which enabled all forms of modernity to be understood as such (and thus denied relativism), as well as enabling cultural variety in terms of the particular inflections of that institutional frame in different socio-political conditions (thus, apparently, denying Euro-triumphalism). What is also significant to note, however, is that European modernity is not understood as split in this way. Rather, it is seen as the originary form of modernity and is presented as the unique combination of the institutional and cultural forms. It is this combined cultural-institutional form that is then further culturally inflected through its interaction with other societies to create *multiple* modernities. Theorists of multiple modernities sidestep the issue of historical inter-connections in the context of the emergence of European modernity – those connections argued for by theorists of underdevelopment and of dependency – and only regard as significant those connections that brought European modernity to other societies. Although, of course, they do not address the actual historical processes of colonialism, enslavement and dispossession; rather these are euphemized under terms such as European contact or mere diffusion.

In this way, theorists of multiple modernities assert the necessary priority of the West in the construction of a comparative sociology of multiple modernities and end up privileging the same under-standing of modern societies as earlier modernization theorists (and as Francis Fukuyama). Although they seek to dissociate themselves from Eurocentrism, they do this at the same time as embracing its core assumptions, namely, 'the Enlightenment assumptions of the centrality of a Eurocentred type of modernity' (Eisenstadt and Schluchter 1998: 5). The triumphalism may no longer be explicitly normative, in that there is a muted 'acceptance' of diverse forms of modernity; it is, however, still embodied within the analytical framework in use. By maintaining a general framework within which varieties of modernity are to be located – and identifying the varieties with culture, and the experience of Europe with the derivation of the general framework itself – theorists of multiple modernities have, in effect, neutralized any challenge that a consideration of other histories could have posed. Thus, theorists of multiple modernities seek to contain challenges to the dominant theoretical framework of sociology by not allowing 'difference' *to make a difference* to what are seen as the original categories of modernity.

Theorists of multiple modernities, in their attempt to rehabilitate modernization theory, then, merely reinforced the deficiencies of that sociological paradigm and introduced further problems; some of which could have been resolved if they had taken seriously the work of earlier scholars within the area of underdevelopment and dependency theory. One of the reasons why they may not have addressed the literature in this area is because their focus was on the Soviet Union and the countries of what had been the Eastern bloc. Eisenstadt, for example, distinguishes the Soviet and Communist societies from those of the Third World and suggests that the Communist societies 'were not simply backward and underdeveloped, aspiring to become modern'; rather, they should be understood as 'modern or modernizing societies' which were now seeking to catch up with the more developed West (1992: 33). It is evident from such a formulation that there is a distinct hierarchy underpinning Eisenstadt's conceptualization of modernity that places Third World countries as backward, Communist societies as modern or modernizing, and Western European and North American societies as developed. Alongside this belief in the advanced character of Western societies, however, there is also unease about whether the turbulence evident in Eastern Europe is confined to the specific problems of 'Communist modernity' or whether it also 'bears witness to some of the problems and tensions inherent in modernity itself' (Eisenstadt 1992: 35; for discussion see Ray 1997). If the latter, this turbulence would be of even greater significance as it would point to 'the potential fragility of the whole project of modernity' (Eisenstadt 1992: 35); if the former, then it could be regarded as opening up 'new terrains of struggle *for* modernity' (Ray 1997: 547).

This concern about the nature and future of modernity is explicit in the writings published in the immediate aftermath of the revolutions in Eastern Europe reflecting uncertainty as to the direction of change they indicated. By the very end of the twentieth century and the beginning of the twenty-first, this concern had dissipated and multiple modernities could be confidently articulated as a paradigm reflecting the ideological and political success of Western modernity. This was notwithstanding that the period since the 1980s was also associated with widening social and economic inequalities and challenges to the 'mixed economies' and welfare regimes that earlier modernization theorists had seen as stable characteristics of a late modernity with the capacity for reform. Even while lip-service was now paid to 'different' forms of being modern, there was a confidence that this difference was not a difference that mattered as the legacy of the great historical and cultural project of modernity, as Wagner (2001) puts it, was now secure even in its revanchist neo-liberal form. While both modernization theory and the radical critiques of underdevelopment theory were concerned with the choice posed between different versions of the modern, with multiple modernities that choice disappeared and was replaced by a differentiation, instead, between the modern and the anti-modern. In the process, colonialism and its associated structures of race are once again displaced from any understanding of that differentiation.

2

From Modernization Theory to World History

The theories of underdevelopment and dependency were not the only criticisms of modernization theory. Even if the latter claimed to be part of a tradition of classical sociology and of Weber in particular, many critics viewed it as a theoretical scheme imposed on the historical record rather than as a genuinely historical sociology. A concern to understand the global differently did not only arise from Marx-inspired theoretical critiques, but also from those who wanted an account that was more sensitive to historical research.

In this chapter I examine three such approaches. The first is the work of historian Fernand Braudel who, in distinguishing between his concern to write a 'world history' from writing the history of the world, contributed to the establishment of a particular tradition of historical social science, or social-scientific history. Within sociology, this tradition was taken up by both Weberian and Marxist sociologists. I look, in turn, at the grand projects of Michael Mann, on charting the sources of social power, and Immanuel Wallerstein, on delineating the modern world system, as exemplary of this idea of a 'world history'.

I

Fernand Braudel's 'world history', published as the three-volume series under the general title, *Civilization and Capitalism, 15th–18th Century*, is explicitly written 'outside the world of theory' and is intended 'to

be guided by concrete observation and comparative history alone'
(Braudel 1981: 25). It is a magisterial study of social and economic
life that builds an argument about the development of global capitalist
economy by drawing together illustrative accounts from around much
of the world. The first two volumes, *The Structures of Everyday Life*
(1981) and *The Wheels of Commerce* (1982), are organized thematically
around understandings of material civilization and market economy.
The third, *The Perspective of the World* (1985), in Braudel's words,
'is a chronological study of the forms and successive preponderant
tendencies of the international economy' (1981: 25). While Braudel,
in reflecting upon the writing of these volumes, says that he does not
claim to have depicted everything about the complex world from the
fifteenth to the eighteenth centuries, he is nonetheless attempting
to assemble various 'scenes' to create a coherent whole (1981: 559).
The framing device that brings unity to this endeavour is an understanding of capitalism as a system, as having developed in Europe and
subsequently diffused around the world to create a world system of
capitalism. What will be at issue is precisely what is held to make up
that system.

Braudel argues that the meta-narrative of capitalism provides
a 'model' that enables both an exposition of European history and
the incorporation of snapshots of history from elsewhere (1985:
619). While Braudel is critical of those economic histories which
focus only on events in Europe, his own volumes are, themselves,
oriented to understanding the dynamics of European history with
other histories only discussed in light of their relationships (usually
subordinate) to Europe. As Braudel states, these volumes constitute
'a long project backwards from the facilities and habits of present-
day life' (1981: 27); that is, Braudel uses the present to select and then
structure the dynamics of the past deemed to be worthy of consideration. It is the present-day understanding of the global, as structured
by a particular form of European dominance, which provides the
basis for the development of the narrative. Thus, while Braudel may
be writing his histories self-consciously 'outside the world of theory',

the commonsensical grand narrative of European capitalist development, or modernity, continues to underpin his assemblage. This grand narrative is so thoroughly embedded within Braudel's cultural framework that it no longer requires explicit acknowledgement; it is presented, instead, 'as the historian's "common sense"' (Weinstein 2005: 77). In this context, I argue that selection is itself a theoretical intervention in the ordering of history as I will discuss in more detail at the end of this chapter.

Braudel distinguishes between an empirical understanding of the world and the analytical use of 'world-', that is, world with a hyphen. While the 'world' is to be understood as pertaining to the *whole* world, 'world-economy', for example, 'only concerns a fragment of the world, an economically autonomous section of the planet … to which its internal links and exchanges give a certain organic unity' (1985: 22). The varieties of world-economies that have existed in the past have, according to Braudel, been worlds unto themselves, not necessarily co-extensive with the world as such.[1] The European world economy is seen to be the first world economy to have world-historical relevance, that is, to have created a *world* economy. It is this belief that underpins the narrative and analytical structure of the volumes whereby examples are drawn from other parts of the world only to the extent that they illuminate some aspect of the European story, that is, 'to form a clearer judgement of Europe' (1985: 387). Even the chapters of Volume 3, explicitly focused on 'the rest of the world', are narrated in terms of the connections of the rest of the world to what are seen as European developments. As Braudel writes, while it might have been preferable to try to understand non-Europe 'on its own terms, it cannot properly

---

[1] Braudel's formulation of different epochs of 'world-economy' is significant. It is doubtful that the latter could be understood without political and social institutions that incorporated the territories of such an economy, in other words, empires. Indeed, most writers, for example, Eisenstadt (1965), identify earlier periods of world-economy as periods of empire. Braudel is concerned with capitalist world-economy and might have been made sensitive to the issue of its political and social institutions by his very recognition of previous phases of world-economy and their connotations with empire. But this was not to be the case.

be understood, even before the eighteenth century, except in terms of the mighty shadow cast over it by western Europe' (1985: 386).

The connections that Braudel recognizes between Europe and the wider world are seen to be central to Europe's development. Indeed, he even asks whether 'Europe's industrial revolution – the key to her destiny – [would] have been possible' without such interactions (1985: 387). However, nowhere in the three volumes does he empirically address the substance of those connections; that is, imperialism, enslavement, dispossession and colonialism. Instead, he talks about 'the discovery of America' (1985: 388), slavery as part of the solution to the problem of a shortage of labour in the Americas, 'India's self-inflicted conquest' (1985: 489) and so on. In discussing the decline of India in the nineteenth century, Braudel wonders whether this was a consequence of 'the peculiar form of capitalism in India' or maybe 'the economic and social straitjacket of a low wage structure?' (1985: 518). Other options were: 'the difficult political situation', 'growing intervention by Europeans', 'India's technological backwardness' or the impact 'of the machine revolution in Europe' (1985: 518). He does, however, consider an alternative explanation as well, 'an external not an internal explanation – in a word, Britain' (1985: 522). Even here, however, the explanations are based in terms of India's loss of trade, of industry, of markets, losses which the English were then able to exploit. 'Ironically,' Braudel writes, 'India's very strength was used to bring about her destruction ... to the greater profit of the English' (1985: 522). Britain's connection to India is seen primarily in terms of being able to exploit India's misfortune with no discussion of how Britain may have been implicated in the creation of that misfortune. While in other contexts, the issue of agency is seen to be central to European activities, here Europe is curiously presented as the passive recipient of good fortune (a consequence of the disassociated misfortune of others).

Braudel ends his chapter on the relations between Europe and the rest of the world by suggesting that 'we still do not really know how this position of superiority was established and above all maintained'

(1985: 533–4). This is stated at the same time as asserting that the Industrial Revolution was not only 'an instrument of development', but that it was also 'a weapon of domination and destruction of foreign competition' (1985: 535). My argument is that if we focus on the latter, we may be closer to understanding the reasons for Europe's dominance in, and over, the world. Throughout Braudel's text there are occasional references to the explanation of Europe's dominance resting in her involvement in the enslavement of Africans and the indigenous populations of the Americas, the appropriation of natural resources from other parts of the world, the destruction of foreign markets to enable the better distribution of her own commodities, the exploitation of technological advances and discoveries made elsewhere, the subjugation of other peoples and so on. These references, however, are fragmentary and are not brought together as part of the system he is seeking to disclose; that is, he fails to establish a systematic explanation based on these connections. Instead, the dynamics of European history are regarded as explainable only in terms of internal forces and the global exists simply as a space into which European activities spill out. There is little consideration of the global as having been meaningfully constituted by the variety of activities, violent conquest as well as mutual trade, which over time knit the world together empirically.

II

Michael Mann's four-volume study, *The Sources of Social Power*, published over the span of a quarter of a century (1986–2013), is organized around what he presents as four key dimensions of power: economic, ideological, military and political. His concern at the outset of the project is to navigate a path between functionalist accounts of modernization, which also operated in terms of four functions (even if they weren't called types of social power), and their dominant alternative as expressed in Marxist critiques of underdevelopment and dependency theory, where equivalent functions were seen to be structured on the dominance of the economic. He suggests that understanding the ways in which social power determines the shape of societies 'is an empirical question' that requires an address to historical evidence from the beginning of human history to the present (1986: 30). Nonetheless, the empirical material is to be organized around the four dimensions of power.

The four dimensions are held to be dimensions of power in order to set out a more realist account of social relations than that found within functionalist modernization theory. Where, in the latter, material factors are associated with two of the functions, economic and political, and only the latter is specifically linked to the category of power, Mann incorporates all four principles as expressions of different kinds of power. From his perspective, on the other hand, the problem with Marxist approaches is that, despite the concern with power, they over-emphasize the economic to the neglect of the other three dimensions. This understanding organizes the first part of the first volume which is designed to establish that, nonetheless, the economic does come to predominance with the rise of capitalist modernity.

Anybody engaging with the vast historical record that is Mann's canvas is necessarily going to be selective. As with Braudel before him, Mann is concerned to stress that he is not necessarily writing a history *of* the world, but rather, drawing upon the most appropriate history, 'that of the most powerful human society', in order to comment *upon* the world (1986: 31). The history of modern Western civilization, he argues, 'has been just about continuous from the origins of Near Eastern civilization around 3000 BC to the present day' (1986: 31) and it is for this reason, together with its status as being the most powerful society, that the history of the world will be told in terms of the history of the West. What the discontinuities are in the histories of other peoples and places is not mentioned; neither, as will be suggested subsequently, is there space for discussion of the historical context in which the West became 'the most powerful human society' on the planet.

The first volume, *A History of Power from the Beginning to AD 1760*, sets out the 'pre-history' of a variety of civilizations from Mesopotamia to Phoenicia, Greece and Rome before looking in more detail at the 'set of interrelated dynamics ... that medieval Europe possessed and that helped it move toward industrial capitalism' (1986: 373).[2] In the selection of histories that make up the first half of the volume, Mann writes that though he has 'not discussed developments in China and India, they would have been recognizably similar to those described so far in the Middle East and the Mediterranean' (1986: 341). Significant differences between societies, he suggests, only emerged in response to challenges from major religions or philosophies such that by AD 1000 'four recognisably different types of society existed, each with its own dynamism and development' (1986: 341). These differences were not to be superseded 'until one of them, Christianity, proved so far superior to the others that all had to adapt to its encroachments, thus becoming a family of societies once more' (1986: 341). Despite the now significant differences identified by Mann between the four, this becomes the basis of, again, not discussing the others as now the differences make global comparative sociology 'too difficult' (1986: 371).[3] First, other parts of the world and other histories were not discussed because of their similarities, then they are not to be discussed because of their differences. Further, in the turn to focusing solely on Europe, any conjunctures 'impinging on Europe from outside' are to be set aside

---

[2] This is remarkably similar to the concentration on different societies found in Parsons's (1966) more straightforwardly, theoretically derived study.

[3] In a similar fashion, Mann acknowledges, in Volume 1, his omission of 'gender relations' (1986: 31) and promises to address this omission in Volume 2. However, in the Introduction to Volume 2, he abandons his 'original intent to focus on gender relations in this volume' citing the fact that gender relations 'have their own history, currently being rewritten by feminist scholarship' (1993: 16). This is not a lot different to his treatment of postcolonial scholarship. Apparently, despite his avowed interest in connections, important histories can be written without impinging on mainstream histories. From most perspectives, the 'rewriting' of histories by feminist and other scholarship would be a moment for pause and reflection about their impact on the histories being written outside their influence. This points to the role of ideal type methodology and the value-relevant concerns of feminists not being the same as his own as a means of disengagement.

(for now), in favour of an endogenous account oriented to detailing the emergence of European 'class-nations' (1986: 373, 495).

The second half of the first volume, then, presents 'essentially a single story', 'the history of a single "society", Europe', told in terms of its systemic dynamism that integrated 'its diversities into one civilization' (Mann 1986: 500, 504). The conjunctures 'impinging on Europe from outside', that were initially flagged to be dealt with in the final chapters, amount effectively to a half-page discussion of Europe's relationship with Islam. While Mann suggests that Europe may have 'borrowed some things from Islam', he suggests that what they were 'is still controversial' and whether they 'made a critical contribution to European development is still unclear' (1986: 508). What is clear, however, is that 'the necessity of military defence' against Islam or the Mongols united the variety of European states 'in the defence of Europe' and thereby 'protected the dynamic through their military-power organizations' (1986: 508).

The only connections explicitly acknowledged by Mann between Europe and the rest of the world involved the defence of Europe against potential 'invaders'. There is little discussion of the actual incursions by Europe into much of the rest of the world: for example, the Spanish conquest of the Americas, the European empires that stretched across the majority of the globe, the European trade in human beings and so forth. This omission continues in the second volume, *The Rise of Classes and Nation States, 1760–1914*, which focuses on primarily endogenous accounts of five Western countries from the Industrial Revolution to the outbreak of the First World War.

The second volume charts the history of the West's geopolitical development by examining how the 'structuring role of nation-states' was 'also entwined with classes' (1993: 33). The exclusive focus on the emergence and development of 'class-nations' reinforces the inter-nalist account characteristic of the first volume and leaves little room for discussion of the ways in which broader political and economic configurations might also have been significant for understanding the developments under discussion. As Tooze writes, '[i]nsofar as the world is allowed to enter, it is by way of global capitalism and then only in a single, sheepish chapter' (2013: 133). Further, for a four-volume study, in which one of the structuring variables is 'military power', there is remarkably little discussion of the exercise of that power by European states within the world and the consequences that this entailed.[4] European colonialism as a significant aspect of the rise of Europe was supposed to be addressed in the third volume, which is oriented specifically to global empires. As Mann himself notes in the preface, this volume, *Global Empires and Revolution, 1890–1945,* was supposed to 'rectify an omission in Volume 2, the neglect of the global empires created by the most advanced countries' (2012: vii). 'These are, of course,' he continues, 'essential for an understanding of modern societies' (2012: vii). The accounts given of empire, however, are largely descriptive and there is little attempt to reconsider the historical narratives or social-scientific claims of the earlier volumes in light of this, given that 1890 is hardly the constitutive moment of European empires.

Volumes 1 and 2 provided an account of the emergence of what, for him, is the most powerful human society, Europe, in terms of internal factors such as the development of 'class-nations' within it. However, the turn to what he regards as 'external factors', those of empire, ought at least to necessitate a reconsideration of the account of 'internal' factors. For a start, it should be recognized that, given that many European states were imperial and colonial states, at the same time as, or even prior to, becoming national states, the formulation 'class-nation' is itself, at best, an initial interpretive device for subsequent reinterpretation and, at worst, simply incorrect. However, Mann's history of the British Empire does little to reinterpret what was previously seen as

---

[4]   As with Braudel, the implicit recognition of the role of military power in the constitution of earlier world-economies and their status as empires might have led him to address its role in establishing and stabilising the very market relations bound up with nation states and classes. A historical sociology attuned to comparative issues might have been expected to rehabilitate the role of military power in the history of the West, including its economic dominance, not further displace it.

'British' industry or the 'British' state. Further, there is a curious failure to address European empires in the *longue durée*, that is, from the Spanish imperialism of the fifteenth century that arguably began the process of creating the world as it came to be known from a European perspective. Mann skips from briefly considering the British Empire to considering the US and Japanese empires, but these latter are discussed primarily in terms of their activities in the twentieth century. By missing out an address of the Spanish, Portuguese, French, Italian and other European empires, Mann does little to re-contextualize or rethink the historical narratives of the preceding volumes. Despite him suggesting that understanding empires is essential for understanding modern societies, and seeking to rectify their omission from earlier volumes, it seems that the arguments made in those earlier volumes do not need to be changed as a consequence of this necessity.

For the most part, the approach to empire in the first three volumes presents it either as a precursor intermediate historical formation to modern capitalism, that is, in terms of a form of political empire, such as Austro-Hungary, that would subsequently fracture to create 'class-nations'; or as an appendage that had little consequence for developments in the 'class-nation' with which it was associated. In the fourth volume, *Globalizations, 1945–2011*, this disassociation goes further with empire primarily being used to describe the form of the US in the late twentieth century. Further, there is little discussion of the impact of processes of decolonization on the 'class-nations' of Europe or the ways in which decolonization fundamentally reshaped Europe and the global order more generally (see Hansen 2002). The failure to address empire adequately in these accounts means that Mann misses its central role in the historical formation of 'class-nations' or their transformation in the period of decolonization.

As Linda Colley (1992, 2002) has argued, it was the existence of empire that enabled the class-settlement in Britain whereby the working-classes and other classes were drawn into and made a part of the national project initially fashioned by elites. This was associated with rising living standards as a consequence of imported food and the rationalization of domestic agriculture, as well as empire providing an opportunity for upward mobility for middle and professional classes. A later welfare state settlement was further facilitated, as Holmwood (2000b) argues, through continuing policies of cheap foodstuffs and commodities, enabled now through a system of Commonwealth preferences. Indeed, in this context, it could be argued that it was decolonization which fractured the class-settlement in Britain after the 1960s, leading to the return of high levels of inequality un-ameliorated by the resources of empire. In displacing the specific histories of European colonialism with general accounts of political empire broadly understood, these volumes fail to acknowledge the interconnections, and their implications, that ensued from colonial relations and continue to impinge on the social structures of domestic formations in the postcolonial period.[5]

The rise of modern capitalism is located in the intertwined development of classes and nations in Europe and the form of modernity is associated with the dominance of economic power. 'Economic imperialism', that is, the expansion of markets and, with them, the diffusion of European influence, including military power, is taken to be the central process in the development of world history. In this way, a teleological account is smuggled into a historiography argued to be profoundly anti-teleological and the economic is privileged in a fourfold scheme in which all aspects are argued to be equally significant. Ironically, Mann's attempt to steer a third way between structural functionalist interpretations and the economic determinism of Marxist critique, leads him to a curious form of Weberian Trotskyism, where historical developments are parsed as uneven and combined development, albeit where development is represented in ideal typical terms

---

[5] In this context, Runciman's three-volume treatise of sociological theory, which ends with a case study of the history of Britain, is significant (Runciman 1997). He argues for the three modes of production, persuasion, and coercion that characterize any society to have been fully established as capitalist, liberal, and democratic respectively by the immediate post-World War One period with no subsequent mutations or challenges to their stability. Once again, colonialism, empire, and its end have no determining significance for understanding English society (for further discussion, see Holmwood 1998).

and the processes derive their character from Weberian sociology rather than that of Marx. Ultimately, as with Eisenstadt and the other modernization theorists before him, modern nation states are formed endogenously in Europe without regard to the imperial and colonial contexts of those states. At the same time, the generalization of nation states in the twentieth century is assigned to the break-up of empires whose substance in the eighteenth and nineteenth centuries has gone largely unrecognized.

The plurality of the 'new combinations' of the political, economic, military and ideological outside European combinations has, of course, the form of multiple modernities. Globalization is a European phenomenon, fractured by disjunctive engagements with it such that European dominance is finally in question, ultimately leaving a primacy of the economic at the core of his argument. The chapter now turns to the more explicit focus on the economy that is found in Wallerstein's world systems theory.

III

Immanuel Wallerstein's project of charting the development of 'the modern world system' is comparable to the works discussed above and, indeed, is closely affiliated with the tradition of historical social science associated with Fernand Braudel (see Smith 1991). Wallerstein is clear that he is not writing a history, but, instead, is seeking 'to describe the world system at a certain level of abstraction, that of the evolution of structures of the whole system' (1974a: 8). In this, he could be regarded as close to Mann's project of providing an historical account of the sources of social power. The substantive and geographical coordinates of Wallerstein's study are also broadly similar to the preceding authors. Chronologically, his study ranges from a medieval prelude to, eventually, the present day; and, spatially, it is predominantly focused on European history and the contemporary West. His is projected to be a six-volume series, with the four published volumes taking us up to the beginnings of the First World War in 1914. There are a further two planned volumes that, he writes in the preface to the fourth volume, will focus on the twentieth century and take us through to 2050, charting the demise of the modern world system and pointing to 'a successor or successors yet unknown' (2011b: xvii).

Where Wallerstein differs from Braudel and Mann is in terms of the explicit intellectual context out of which his study emerges; that is, in his explicit advocacy for a Marxist-inspired interpretation of world history. Wallerstein was involved in the debates around dependency and underdevelopment, discussed in the previous chapter, but believed them to be insufficient to address the systematic nature of capitalism in operation in the contemporary world (see Wallerstein 1974b). A further distinction was that his early work was situated in an attempt to understand processes of colonial rule, decolonization and independence in Africa in the mid twentieth century, albeit within a broadly functionalist perspective. In seeking the appropriate unit of analysis to study the post-independence countries, he suggests that he was forced to turn his 'attention to early modern Europe' and to scale-up from sovereign states and national societies to the world system (1974a: 6–7). The latter was because only the world system constituted a social system within which all constituent elements could be located and related; and the former because Europe was understood to be 'the origins and early conditions of the world-system' (1974a: 10). In this way, his understanding of the historical emergence of modern capitalism was closely related to his establishment of the world system as the social-scientific unit of analysis appropriate for explaining that emergence and both were arrived at from an initial starting point rooted in his academic work on Africa. However, as will become apparent, Africa subsequently disappears from his delineation of the world systems model which is focused primarily on an understanding of European nation state history.[6]

---

[6]   In the preface to Volume 4, Wallerstein (2011b: xvi) writes that he plans to address 'the

In very basic terms, and drawing on his first volume, Wallerstein's modern world system can be understood as follows. The long sixteenth century saw the emergence of a European world economy that was a system of economic linkages greater than any juridically defined political unit. It was distinguished from empires, which were regarded as political units, and differed from earlier world-economies precisely by not being also transformed into empires. Instead, the European world economy 'embarked on the path of capitalist development which enabled it to outstrip these others' (1974a: 17). Capitalism, according to Wallerstein, is only feasible within a world economy and not a world-empire, although he does not provide an analytical account of why this might be so. Instead, he simply follows Weber in comparing China with Europe and outlines the distinctions between them. These distinctions are then used to explain, retrospectively, Europe's turn to capitalism and China's failure or inability to do so.

As with Weber before him, Wallerstein presents China as having the material conditions for capitalism in the early modern period, but failing to develop capitalism in the modern period. 'It is doubtful', he writes, 'that there was any significant difference between Europe and China in the fifteenth century on certain base points: population, area, state of technology (both in agriculture and in naval engineering). To the extent that there were differences it would be hard to use them to account for the magnitude of the difference of development in the coming centuries' (1974a: 62). He departs from Weber, however, by arguing further that the difference in value systems, to which Weber had attributed explanatory purchase, 'seems both grossly exaggerated and, to the extent that it existed, once again [does] not account for the different consequences' (1974a: 62). The essential difference, for Wallerstein, rested in 'the conjuncture of a secular trend', going back to the ancient empires of Rome and China, 'with a more immediate economic cycle', whereby Europe moved towards cattle and wheat and China towards rice (1974a: 63). Nowhere does he discuss the

scramble for Africa and the rise of movements of national liberation' in Volume 5.

possibility that the causes of the 'divergence' may (also) have rested in the impact of British commercial and foreign policy towards China, over the eighteenth and nineteenth centuries. The extent of Wallerstein's consideration of the issue is summed up in the following sentences: 'with the Treaty of 1842, China would start on the path of being herself incorporated. But that is another story' (2011a: 168). Expanding a little on this story, most historians agree that the fundamental problem for the British in terms of their trade with China was that the Chinese did not wish to purchase anything that the British produced, preferring instead to trade their goods only for bullion. This changed when Britain realized that it could use the resources of India, namely tea and opium, to finance its investment in China, despite the fact that China prohibited the import of the latter (Greenberg 1951; Dean 1976). The illicit supply of opium into China was initially tacitly authorized by the British government and then explicitly so through the Opium Wars which forced China to open up her markets to international trade as well as to grant extraterritorial rights to British traders within her borders, without, of course, any reciprocal rights for Chinese traders in British markets (O'Brien and Pigman 1992). British gunboat diplomacy, or 'free-trade imperialism' (Gallagher and Robinson 1953), was the means by which Britain was able to extend the markets within which she was able to sell her goods. As Greenberg (1951) has argued, large-scale production at home meant producing more than the domestic market could absorb, thereby creating the need to sell the surplus abroad. So, a key part of the explanation of British economic dynamism is not an endogenous story but, rather, a story of colonial dimensions. Nowhere does Wallerstein discuss these aspects as potentially integral aspects of the explanation for why China did not develop to capitalism in a manner similar to Europe.[7]

One of the reasons for this can be seen more clearly in his separation of the two main elements that he suggests are constitutive of the

---

[7] Interestingly, Kenneth Pomeranz (2000), in his book *The Great Divergence*, also has but a single reference to the Opium Wars and attributes little significance to 'gunboat diplomacy' in his account of the making of a singular world economy.

modern world system: 'the capitalist world-economy … built on a worldwide division of labour' and 'political action [that] occurred primarily within the framework of states' (1974a: 162; for discussion, see Robinson 2011). While he recognizes that the economic linkages between places were appropriately understood in the context of the world, he circumscribes the remit of political action to that of the national state. But the very context for a worldwide division of labour that included slavery and coerced cash-crop labour, sharecropping, bonded labour, and free labour was usually an imperial or colonial regime that participated in enslavement and subjugation beyond its national boundaries. Further, as discussed above, the worldwide free market was not necessarily 'freely' created but emerged as a consequence of coercion, warfare and subjugation of other powers. That is, the realm of political action extended beyond the national state and was constituted in the imperial or colonial states within which 'worldwide' economic differentiation was created and managed. By distinguishing a world economy from an ideal type of world-empire, Wallerstein has little room in his analysis for the very real empires of European states, or the 'free-trade imperialism' they operated, that had worldwide reach. Where these are discussed, they are discussed in terms of their peripheral relation to the European world economy (the Americas) or as external to it (Asia) (1974a: 336) and the manner of their 'incorporation' is naturalized (as above, 'China would start on the path of being herself incorporated' (2011a: 168)).

Introducing his chapter on incorporation, Wallerstein writes: 'Incorporation into the capitalist world-economy was never at the initiative of those being incorporated. The process derived from the need of the world economy to expand its boundaries, a need which was itself the outcome of pressures internal to the world-economy' (2011a: 129). Here, he acknowledges there were pressures that preceded expansion and that expansion was forced upon others, but he does not name the processes that facilitated this: colonialism and imperialism. Wallerstein consistently euphemizes European colonial and imperial history within his history of the modern world system understood in terms of capitalism. He writes, for example, that 'the discovery of America was to give Europe a richer source of gold than the Sudan and especially a far richer source of silver than central Europe' and suggests that 'the economic consequences [of this] would be great' (1974a: 41). There is no mention of the processes of colonialism, dispossession or appropriation (or, more simply, theft) that enabled Europe to have access to those precious metals and to use them for her development alone and, in the process, create the conditions for the underdevelopment of others (see Trouillot 2003; Goody 2006; Hobson 2004).

Wallerstein discusses this process in a little more depth in the second volume, but even here naturalizes what other scholars have documented as an exceedingly brutal process (Bakewell 1971; Galeano 1973; Cole 1985; Brown 2012). Wallerstein writes, 'the Europeans first seized Inca gold, then mined Potosi and Mexican silver ... They sent settlers to control the area of the Americas politically and to supervise the economic operations, and they imported labor as well. In short, they incorporated the Americas into their world-economy' (1980: 109). This rather glosses over the violence and force necessary in seizing Inca gold, the coerced and enslaved labour required to mine the silver, the forced transportation of human beings from one part of the world to work for Europeans in another part of the world. Further, the European world economy is seen to have its own internal logic and the only consequence of wider engagements is the transformation and incorporation of peripheral or external areas into it; there is no discussion of how the European world economy, or our understanding of it, may have changed in turn. It also fails to address the analytical significance of the incorporation that is recognized. Namely, that the incorporation of the Americas into the European world economy was not based on freely chosen market relations.

Given that, for Wallerstein, the market, and the free relations this assumes, was central to the establishment of a specifically capitalist form of world economy, acknowledgement of 'unfree' incorporation seriously undermines the theoretical claims otherwise made. He states quite straightforwardly that 'capitalism as an economic mode is based on the fact that the economic factors operate within an arena larger than that which any political entity can totally control' (1974a: 348). This, he continues, 'gives capitalists a freedom of maneuver that is structurally based' and that 'has made possible the constant economic expansion of the world-system, albeit a very skewed distribution of its rewards' (1974a: 348). It is clear, however, that colonial expansion preceded capitalist relations, given that the latter were created and maintained through colonial violence. Further, Wallerstein's recognition of the 'skewed distribution of its rewards' points to an acknowledgement of hierarchies other than ones created through the market, but nowhere is this integrated into his broader theoretical analysis.

In another instance, in discussing the increase in the land area under European control and the favourable land/labour ratio this brought about, Wallerstein does not refer to colonization and dispossession as the basis of this. He simply points to the existence of 'formal overseas colonies of European powers' as if this was a natural fact that did not require explanation (1974a: 68). 'Europe expanded into the Americas', Wallerstein writes (1974a: 128); with no discussion of the 'double conquest' this entailed, that is, whereby the earlier inhabitants of the continent 'lost not only sovereignty, but commons and severalty also' (Jennings 1971: 541). In his second volume, Wallerstein answers the question of how one 'creates' a market in a particular place, 'if there aren't enough people of a high enough income level' there, with the suggestion that 'one encourages "settlement"' (1980: 239). The appropriation of land en masse in the Americas by European migrants, or settler-colonists, not only improved the land/labour ratio for Europeans, but it also, as Wallerstein argues, 'made possible the large-scale accumulation of basic capital which was used to finance the rationalisation of agricultural production' (1974a: 69). Again, instead of focusing on the processes of colonization that enabled this, Wallerstein moves to address 'the so-called price revolution' which, he suggests, is central to historiographical debates on the topic (1974a: 69). With these two examples, we see the way in which the empirical record pointing to the importance of colonial relations is subsumed to a consideration of the pre-formed theoretical debates on the emergence of capitalism.

IV

The first two chapters have sought to examine the ways in which ideas of the global developed within sociology in the twentieth century. The first chapter focused on how different sociological traditions, such as Weberian modernization theory or Marxist underdevelopment theory, worked with an implicit understanding of the global in the construction of the societal types that were seen to be the basis of their theoretical models. This chapter, in turn, examined the construction of the global in the work of those sociologists who engaged directly with the historical record. Despite their many theoretical and methodo-logical differences, what is clear is the extent of common agreement on a particular narrative concerning the emergence of the global. This is a narrative that, simply put, asserts the singular importance of European history from the medieval period onwards and develops its understanding of the global in terms of subsuming all other events and narratives to the one emerging from Europe.

Modernization theory avows the singular achievement of Europe and the West and holds up this experience as the model for the rest of the world. Underdevelopment and dependency theory, for the most part, critique the celebratory aspect of the modernization narrative and argue for the development of alternatives to liberal capitalism. They do not, however, contest the historical adequacy of the narra-tives underpinning the theoretical framework of modernization. The conceptual paradigm of multiple modernities, similarly, critiques the idea of a singular path to modernity, but does not disagree with the historical understanding concerning the emergence of, what is believed to be, European modernity. History, in the first chapter, is not directly engaged with, but simply confirms what is already known. In the second chapter, the historical record is addressed directly, but here the issue of selection operates to maintain agreement on one particular narrative.

The difficulty with attempting to understand the world, or the idea of the global, historically is determining the parameters of the study (for a fuller discussion, see Bhambra 2011b). As Christian (2003) argues, world history, to be meaningful (and possible), has to be more than an encyclopaedic endeavour to document all the histories of all the peoples in the world; what is needed is a particular narrative to bring these histories within a coherent structure. The issue, as McNeill has also suggested, is less about discovering new histories about others, more about ordering them in such a way as 'to present the different facets and interacting flows of human history as we now under-stand them' (1990: 21). The most frequently used structure, or grand narrative, is some version of Weber's 'rise of the West' thesis whether that is organized in terms of models based around understandings of capitalism, power, modernity, or, latterly, globalization. Even positions ostensibly critical of Weberian social science, such as those of under-development and dependency, generally present an historical narrative in terms of expansion outward from an initial transformation, that of feudal Europe into a capitalist world economy. In this way, world systems theory can be understood as following the standard historical trajectory of attributing significance to events which are seen to be endogenously European and which then diffuse out to the world.

The trail laid by Max Weber in seeking to determine the causes of the miracle *of* Europe has been adapted by subsequent scholars attempting to account for the miracle *in* Europe. This can be seen to be the central concern of the projects of both Braudel and Mann discussed above; and while Wallerstein's focus is more on understanding the development of capitalism, his turn to history is similarly oriented to examining the specificities of Europe that, he believes, enabled its world economy to become a truly world-historical one. The social-scientific frames of modernity, power, and capitalism rely on a remarkably similar historical narrative and similar omissions of histories that could have been addressed but were not. McNeill, a historian, suggests that while his personal idiosyncrasies may have previously led him to look at 'history from the point of view of the winners', we must nonetheless acknowledge that point of view and 'admire those who pioneered the enterprise and treat the human adventure on earth as an amazing success story, despite all the suffering entailed' (1990: 3). Questions of who this 'we' consists of, and whether 'we' must celebrate the successes (of some) despite the suffering (of others) entailed by a purportedly inclusive human adventure, formed the nub of postcolonial, and other, criticisms that are the broader impetus for this book.

Part Two

Social Sciences and Questions of Epistemology

3

Opening the Social Sciences
to Cosmopolitanism?

The interest in globalization within the social sciences has not only been about mapping the changes wrought by globalizing processes, but has also been concerned with the consequences of a proper recognition that such changes have occurred and therefore altered the landscape in which social science is conducted. From research seeking to 'demonstrate' the emergence and development of globalization, scholars have become more concerned with addressing the impact of globalization upon disciplinary structures and the possibilities for knowledge production in a global age. The central issue, for many social scientists, appears to rest in the following claim: that as we have moved from a system of nation states to a global system, our conceptual categories are still tied to a nation state framework and thereby are inadequate to address the new phenomena associated with the global age. The world has moved on, but our categories for understanding that world haven't. We are urged by Robinson, among many others, 'to shift our focus from the nation-state as the basic unit of analysis to the global system as the appropriate unit' (1998: 562). This is necessary, he argues, as the earlier paradigms 'are unable to account for mounting anomalies brought about by globalization' and what is required now is an 'epistemological break' (1998: 565, 572). This has been articulated most forcefully over the last decade by Ulrich Beck, with his advocacy of a cosmopolitan social science, and follows an earlier exhortation by Immanuel Wallerstein and colleagues to 'open the social sciences'.

Wallerstein does not depart significantly from Beck in his historical account of the development of the social sciences. Similar to Beck, he regards the social sciences as 'creatures', if not 'creations', of the sovereign territories otherwise known as nation states, 'taking their boundaries as crucial social [and analytic] containers' (Wallerstein *et al.* 1996: 27). As we shall see, he also concurs with the temporalization of Beck's 'first age of modernity' thesis and with the idea that there is a crisis within this age that is bringing into being a different second age. Where they do disagree, however, is that while Beck believes the state-centred paradigms to be adequate for their times (in the nineteenth century of nation states), Wallerstein, arguing for a world system that is at least 500 years old, sees the limits of these state-centred paradigms both in their own time and for ours. In contrast to Beck's call for a cosmopolitan sociology adequate to the present, then, Wallerstein puts forward the idea of 'world systems' analysis as a way of addressing the contemporary limitations of 'nineteenth-century paradigms' as well as their limitations in their own time. In the last chapter, I addressed some of the limitations of Wallerstein's historical conception of the world system and in this chapter I will show how those limitations also figure in his conception of issues of the present and of current disciplinary structures.

I

In the collective history of the social sciences written under his leadership, Wallerstein argues that the social sciences are an enterprise of the modern world. They come into existence at the same time as the circumnavigations of the globe in the late fifteenth and sixteenth centuries begin to establish the finitude of the world as a central feature of European thought. While traditional histories of the social sciences locate their emergence solely with the rise of the state, here Wallerstein and his colleagues point also, albeit in passing, to the importance of the emerging understanding of the global (and Europe's role in constructing this global). This aspect, however, is theorized less systematically than the rise of the modern state in the eighteenth century and its consolidation in the nineteenth. It is this latter that is seen to provide the more immediate context for the 'disciplinarization and professionalization of knowledge, that is to say … the creation of permanent institutional structures designed both to produce new knowledge and to reproduce the producers of knowledge' (1996: 7). The disaggregation of fields of study – disciplines – took place within the territorial limits of the state and the state in turn shaped the contours of the disciplines. This strong association between states and disciplines meant that as scholars began to theorize the changing nature of the state this would come to have serious implications for their understanding of disciplines as well.

The post-Second World War period is seen to be particularly significant in terms of the changes that were taking place 'in the world' and their subsequent implications on the production of knowledge of that world. Wallerstein and colleagues suggest that there were three key phenomena that need to be taken into account. The first was 'the change in the world political structure' brought about by the establishment of the US and USSR as the two super-powers 'and the historical reassertion of the non-European peoples of the world' (1996: 33). The second was the largest population expansion known in the history of the world, and a concomitant expansion in productive capacity. This related to the third key development which they articulated as the 'quantitative and geographic expansion of the university system everywhere in the world' (1996: 33–4). These material factors were seen to impinge on the very modes of knowledge production and also, in time, to require new ways of knowing the world. As Wallerstein *et al.* argue, the disciplines had been organized around two main axes – between the modern and the non-modern world; and, within the modern world, between the past and present – and around three substantive areas of research – the market, the state and civil society (1996: 36). Developments in the latter half of the twentieth century, as outlined above, called into question this earlier disciplinary settlement and criticism coalesced, in particular, around the 'Eurocentric' nature of the social sciences.

Wallerstein *et al.* (1996: 51–2) suggest that it is not surprising that the nineteenth century social sciences were Eurocentric, given the history of European conquest, nor that the cultural universality ascribed to Western ideas came to be seriously questioned in the 1970s concomitant with the growing economic power of East Asia and the perceived threat that this posed to the West. The increasing economic and political presence of other parts of the world, they suggest, also had an impact on reshaping the dominant social-scientific paradigms. The consensus around modernization theory, for example, perhaps the exemplar theory of the first age of modernity, began to break down in the 1960s and 1970s as a consequence of two particular challenges. The first came from feminist and anti-colonial scholars who critiqued the self-asserted universality of the dominant paradigms and demanded the 'opening up', or decolonizing, of the social sciences. This challenge, Wallerstein et al. (1996: 54) argue, was both epistemological as well as political in that it was as much about the personnel within departments as it was about the presuppositions built into theoretical reasoning. The second challenge was that posed by the emergence of 'cultural studies' and the space it opened up for the expression of otherwise minority voices and positions within academic contexts.

For Wallerstein and his colleagues, it was 'real world' crises that brought the limits of the nineteenth-century paradigms into sharp relief. In addition, the shift in action from the state level 'to action at global and local levels' further undermined the claim of 'the self-evident nature of states as conceptual containers' (1996: 83) and challenged the easy association between states and disciplines. These two developments pointed to the inadequacies, both historical and conceptual, of the nineteenth-century paradigms and opened up space for the articulation of different histories and analyses. After clarifying the history of the social sciences, Wallerstein et al. sought 'to elucidate a series of basic intellectual questions about which there has been much recent debate' and to suggest a better way forward (1996: 94). The restructuring of the social sciences, as they envisaged it, took into account contemporary changes in the world and sought to address the politics of knowledge production manifest in the critiques of the dominant paradigms as well as the question of differential resource allocation, globally and across disciplines. The call 'to open the social sciences', then, was also a call for 'the transformation of the power relationships which created the particular form of institutionalization *of* the social sciences' (1996: 56, emphasis added).

While there is much to admire and laud in this project, the strong critique of the social sciences at the outset dissipates by the end of the analysis. This is, in part, a consequence of the failure to clarify and distinguish between 'decolonizing' the social sciences and 'opening' them. While the critique is based on the inadequacy of the association between state and discipline, there is little discussion of what the implications of this are for how we might rethink, and reconfigure, disciplinary constructions historically as well as into the future. The restructuring of the social sciences that the Report ends by advocating is one that calls for us to do social science differently in the future. To the extent that there is little discussion about how a reconceptualized history would be necessary to provide us with the tools for thinking differently in the future, the implication remains that this can be a voluntaristic move or then one that reproduces the inadequacies of the earlier paradigms (indeed, Burawoy (2005a), for one, sees the call as a form of renewed positivism). This is largely because the critique of the historical formation of the social sciences is left simply as that – critique of past practices to be resolved through new objects of inquiry without sufficient consideration of how those past practices continue to inform contemporary disciplinary approaches to supposedly new objects. A thorough-going address of this, as Mignolo (2014) has force-fully argued, would require any opening of the social sciences to be concomitant upon their decolonization. Wallerstein *et al.* do temper the focus on the nation state through their recognition of Europe's dominion over much of the rest of the world, but, I would suggest, this is not properly theorized or discussed within the Report. As Lander has similarly argued, '[i]t is not the same to assume that the historical patrimony of the social sciences is parochial, as to conclude that it is colonial: the implications are drastically different' (1997: 72). What a decolonized social science might look like, then, will be further addressed in the conclusion to this book.

II

Independent of the Report of the Gulbenkian Commission, Wallerstein had outlined his own alternative to the nineteenth-century paradigms under the frame of 'world systems analysis', as discussed in the previous chapter. This mode of enquiry offers both a different historical account of the emergence of the state system as well as a different conceptual framework within which to understand the processes under consideration. While Wallerstein suggests that world systems analysis is not a new paradigm for historical sociology, but rather 'a call for a debate about the paradigm' (2001: 256), there is, nonetheless, a strong methodological and analytical component at its core. Broadly, world systems analysis is defined by a particular relation of space and time; that is, 'the space of a "world" and the time of a "long duration"' (Wallerstein 2001: 267). There is a further specificity, however, which is the definition of the contemporary capitalist world economy as a central aspect of world systems analysis. The intention of world systems analysis is to move beyond the nineteenth-century paradigms in three ways. First, to interrogate theoretically the tripartite division of social-scientific concerns along the lines of the economy, politics and the socio-cultural and to reconstruct these within a uni-disciplinary framework. Second, to address the methodological implications of epistemology being firmly located 'in the swampy middle ground of a historical system' (2001: 271). And, third, to begin to embed these forms of knowledge and ways of knowing within new organizational and institutional forms (Wallerstein 2001: 271–2). The following section discusses the extent to which this has been successful.

Standard historical-sociological accounts of the emergence of the state system suggest processes of internal differentiation and nationalist.[1] He argues that disciplines such as sociology and political science have been historically bound to nation states in their emergence and development such that they are no longer adequate to the task of dealing with the problems and processes that emerge at the level of the 'global'. He highlights the increasing number of social processes that extend beyond national boundaries and suggests that, as a consequence, 'world society' should now be the starting point of sociological and other research (see also Walby 2009). His argument is based on a perceived transition from a process of singular 'modernization' to one giving rise to coexisting 'multiple modernities'. This shift is understood by Beck as a shift from the first age of modernity – that is, one shaped by nation states – to a second, global cosmopolitan, age. While Beck generally follows the multiple modernities paradigm, discussed in an earlier chapter, his call for a *second age* of modernity, and what follows from this, is distinct and, I will go on to argue, contradictory.

In this second age, Beck argues, not only is modernity now multiple, but the concepts which had been in use in developing sociological understandings in the first age are insufficient. They are, he suggests, 'zombie' categories, that is, categories that continue to live in academic discourse even when the world that had initially given rise to them is no longer in existence. Instead, what is needed is a new set of categories and concepts that would emerge from reflection upon this cosmopolitan second age. While I have also argued that sociological concepts are inappropriately bounded – specifically, that they are 'methodologically Eurocentric', rather than methodologically nationalist – this is not something that is *only now* becoming problematic as a supposedly 'first modernity' has given way to a contemporary now-globalized world. Such an approach, I suggest, is as limited as the state-centred approaches under criticism as it is based on the idea that the concepts of the first age of modernity were appropriate to that age and that the only problem is with their application to the present and the future (for discussion, see Chernilo 2007; Fine 2007). At a minimum, however,

---

[1] The following two sections are a modified version of the argument in Bhambra (2011c).

the 'first age of modernity' was as much characterized by empires as by nation states and so the concepts of that age would, by that token, be as inadequate in their own time as they are claimed to be today.

Another significant problem with Beck's call for more appropriate sociological concepts is that his version of cosmopolitanism is at odds with the global age he describes. To the extent that multiple modernities, as the contemporary condition of the global world, are predicated on cultural inflections of modernity, then the world has to be understood as a multicultural world. The place of others within his new cosmopolitan global age, however, is not straightforward given his otherwise stringent critique of multiculturalism.

According to Beck, multiculturalism asserts a world of variety and plurality while at the same time presenting humanity as a collectivity divided on cultural grounds. Individuals within this conception, he continues, are seen as the product of their own languages, traditions, customs and landscapes and have an attachment to their homeland which 'is regarded as a closed, self-sufficient and sacrosanct unity' (2002: 36–7). This entails a defence of that homeland 'naturally' against imperialism, but also, he suggests, against 'miscegenation, internationalization, and cosmopolitanism' (2002: 37).[2] This leads to the conclusion, without any substantiation, that 'multiculturalism is at loggerheads with individualization' and that, within multiculturalism, 'the individual does not exist', being simply an 'epiphenomenon of his culture' (2002: 37). In contrast, cosmopolitanism, Beck suggests, 'argues the reverse and *presupposes* individualization' (2002: 37). However, he does not elaborate on how a cosmopolitanism of individuals is accommodated within a vision of the world as otherwise structured by different cultures. Given that cosmopolitanism must also be a cultural

---

[2] This attribution is ironic not least because the term 'cosmopolitan' was used in European discourse to indicate the 'deracinated' foreigner – frequently, 'the Jew' – whose allegiance to national state formations and political communities could not be guaranteed. Indeed, these concerns are much more characteristic of the 'imperial homelands' of Europe than they are of supposed 'homelands' resisting European imperialism. Beck is concerned with the nationalism of 'others', but does not see its relation to empire as both internal to it and its legacy.

without providing any information on why this must be case. Further, there is little explanation about what makes global elites specifically *cosmopolitan*, while these immigrants are only *transnational*. Beck's patronizing attitude towards these 'poor immigrants' continues a few lines along when he says that: 'it is not only the global players who are learning the de-territorialized game of power and putting it to the test, but also some *ethnic minorities*' (2002: 33). 'Global players' are not, in Beck's understanding, 'ethnic minorities' and 'ethnic minorities' are not 'global players'; the Eurocentrism implicit in the identification of 'global players' is apparent.

V

Beck's (2000; 2006) argument for cosmopolitan social science and Wallerstein's world systems theory are each part of a long line of social theory that takes Western perspectives as the focus of global processes, and Europe as the origin of a modernity which is subsequently globalized, whether in convergent (modernization), divergent (multiple modernities) forms, or expanded world systems. While Beck presents his version of cosmopolitanism as potentially globally inclusive, it is an inclusivity that is dependent upon 'them' being included in 'our' understandings, as is Wallerstein's 'opening' of the social sciences. In neither case, is global knowledge addressed as a de-colonized knowledge. It is not an inclusivity that recognizes others as already constitutive of, if marginalized within, the frameworks of understanding. Nor is it one that sees that there might be something to learn from engagements with others such that those frameworks of understanding might be changed. As such, it can be seen to embody an unmitigated form of cultural Eurocentrism. Further, while Beck uses the approach of multiple modernities to present the distinctiveness of the present age, he does not deal with the contradiction this poses for his commitment to his version of cosmopolitanism. Multiple modernities, as argued previously, are predicated on an understanding of

different cultures such that their vision of the global has to be constituted as a form of global multiculturalism. To the extent that Beck sets
up cosmopolitanism in opposition to multiculturalism he denies the
basis for the very global age he describes.

The problems identified here are not necessarily problems with
the idea of cosmopolitanism itself, but rather with the particularly
parochial understanding of it as presented by Beck. In contrast to
his Eurocentred universalism, and that of Wallerstein, alike, Pollock
et al. (2000), for example, argue for an understanding of cosmopolitanism made up of dialogues among a series of local perspectives on
it. Their primary argument is that the very phenomenon of cosmopolitanism is threatened by the work of purification that insists on
regarding it as the product of one culture, emerging from a centre
and incorporating others in its diffusion outwards. If we wish an
inclusive cosmopolitanism, it would have to be one outside a centred
universalism and one established on the basis of 'connections', both
historical and social. As such, cosmopolitanism would have to be
understood as open and not pre-given in form or content: it is not,
they argue, 'some known entity existing in the world, with a clear
genealogy from the Stoics to Immanuel Kant, that simply awaits more
detailed description at the hands of scholarship' (2000: 577). Rather, it
is best established by looking at 'how people have thought and acted
beyond the local' (2000: 586), in different places and across time, to
generate new descriptions. These would, in turn, suggest new practices,
including new social-scientific practices in ways of understanding the
world.[4] If, as they argue, we were to take cosmopolitanism as *a way of
looking at the world*, this would require us to take the perspective *of
the world* in our considerations; that is, we would need to be cosmopolitan in our very practices in understanding what it was and is to

---

[4]   See Lamont and Aksartova (2002) for one example in which this has been successfully
      undertaken. Acknowledging that much of the literature on cosmopolitanism is either
      implicitly or explicitly associated with elites, they seek 'to explore ordinary cosmo-
      politanisms, defined as the strategies used by ordinary people to bridge boundaries with
      people who are different from them' (2002: 1).

be cosmopolitan. A cosmopolitan social science, then, would be one that was open to different voices. Further, it would be one that provincialized European understandings, not one that continued to assert the necessary hegemony of Europe.

The key issue with both Wallerstein and Beck is that their identification of the limitations of earlier social-scientific paradigms does not lead to the reconstruction of those paradigms. There is little acknowledgement in Beck's work, for example, that if certain understandings are seen as problematic today, then, there must also be an issue of whether they were not also problematic in the past. Most importantly, they would lead to misunderstandings of the nature of the present in terms of how it has arisen from that past. Indeed, any idea of a disjunction between past and present, such that the present represents a new 'phase', is open to the possible objection that there are unrecognized continuities and that the appearance of discontinuity is an artefact of the misunderstanding of past processes and their projected futures. As such, the limitations of nineteenth-century concepts of the first age of modernity require a more thorough address than Beck proposes in his simple shift to a cosmopolitan second age if the requirements of a 'global' sociology are to be properly addressed. Beyond Wallerstein's world systems analysis and Beck's cosmopolitan social science, there have been other ways in which scholars in the contemporary period have attempted to think about both the global context within which the social sciences operate and the social-scientific understandings of the global. The following chapter addresses developments within the International Sociological Association that attempt to do just that.

4

Global Sociology: Indigenous, Subversive, Autonomous?

The idea of 'global sociology' has recently been promoted as a way in which sociology can redress its previous neglect of those represented as 'other' in its construction of modernity. While there is little consensus on the meaning of 'global', either in its own terms or in the context of it as a qualifier of the way in which sociology as a discipline operates (or might come to operate), the standard understanding is as follows. The global, as descriptor, points to the contemporary world order, usually post the 1970s, in which the intensification of worldwide processes under neo-liberal policies has brought more of humanity into contact with each other. The global, as qualifier, points to the need for sociology to engage meaningfully with the world beyond the West. This engagement usually takes one of two forms. First, an argument that the distilled truths of sociology continue to remain valid, but it would be useful for them to be supplemented by additional data from other places. And, second, that what is needed is the inclusion of other voices and other knowledges and thus an expanded canon of sociology and sociological perspectives. Both approaches, in their different ways, are 'additive' and regard the global, and global sociology, as constituted by the steady accretion of new data, neglected theorists and alternative discourses. On this understanding, the global and global sociology are descriptors of the present and a call for sociology to be different in the future. This chapter, and the following one, address the different ways in which sociologists have envisaged the development of global sociology.

The International Sociological Association (ISA), both through its meetings and its journals, has provided an important space for the articulation and wider dissemination of ideas of 'global sociology' from scholars based in locations other than Europe and the US. A journal of the Association, the aptly named *International Sociology*, was described by Martin Albrow, one of its early editors, as a forum for the discussion of 'a global sociological consciousness' and a marker of the development of sociology as an international discipline (1990: 5). The 1980s, for example, saw extensive debate on the possibilities for the 'indigenization' of the social sciences, centred on the arguments of Akinsola Akiwowo (1986, 1988), and the relationship between indigenization and the internationalization of sociology. This was followed in subsequent decades with discussion around the development of autonomous social science traditions, as put forward by Syed Hussein Alatas (2002, 2006), and the need to recognize multiple, globally diverse, origins of sociology. This chapter will focus on these early debates that subsequently coalesced around a call for 'global sociology', both within the journal and more broadly, and discuss the significance of their interventions in this regard.

I

The publication of Akiwowo's 'Contributions to the Sociology of Knowledge from an African Oral Poetry' in the signal journal of the ISA in 1986 caused somewhat of a stir. It proclaimed the importance of indigenizing the sociological enterprise and sought to demonstrate how this could be achieved by extrapolating sociological propositions through an interpretation of the transcribed verses of a Yoruba oral poem (translated into English). The article followed an earlier symposium organized by Akiwowo at the 1982 ISA World Congress on 'Universalism versus Indigenisation in Sociological Theory' from which a number of articles were brought together by him and published in the June 1988 issue of *International Sociology*.

In the editorial introduction, Akiwowo (1988) outlines the intellectual rationale framing his call for the indigenization of the sociological enterprise in terms of three key issues. The first concerns 'the extent to which the conceptual schemes and propositions which constitute mainstream sociological theories, can be accepted as containing universal principles for the explanation of human societies every-where' (1988: 155). The second, focuses on whether sociological theories arising from empirical studies on Western societies can be valid and reliable when used to understand social life and social problems in other places. Third, and conversely, Akiwowo poses the question of the extent to which 'generalisations from empirical studies from Third World societies [can] be accepted and extended to European and American societies' (1988: 155).

The project of indigenization, for him, is not simply a project of recovering and highlighting the cultural resources of societies beyond those which regularly feature within mainstream sociology. It is also a call to address the adequacy of all theories by subjecting them to 'tests and retests within different societal contexts' in order to determine their *empirical* universal validity (1988: 155). While Akiwowo does not use the term *empirical* universal validity, it is clear that he is distinguishing his project of constructing universal claims on the basis of an assessment of their reliability and validity in 'universal' (global?) contexts and not just on the basis of a claim to be so, as, he argues, has been the case for the majority of universalist theories to date. Indigenization, as he articulates it, requires 'the study, analysis and explanation' of society which takes into account the multitude of factors contributing to its constitution and uses all available resources in the endeavour; this includes using the resources of Western 'notions, ideas and thoughts' (1988: 158). Akiwowo's project of indigenization, then, is not an assertion of the radical particularity of specific cultures. Rather, it is a call for learning from the traditions of various cultures in order to develop, through a process of investigation and argument-ation, universal propositions and frameworks that are adequate for the task in a variety of locations.

The focus of Akiwowo's scholarship on developing sociological propositions from the traditions of Yoruba oral poetry caused a certain degree of disquiet among both fellow sociologists in Nigeria and those further afield. Most prominently, perhaps, his call for indigenization was addressed by Margaret Archer (1991), in her Presidential Address to the World Congress, where she critiqued the move within sociology toward fragmentation and localization in the context of society itself moving in the direction of globalization and greater integration. With the title of her address, 'Sociology for One World: Unity and Diversity', Archer proceeded to map 'the irony of an increasingly global society which is met by an increasingly localised sociology' (1991: 132). In the face of the radical relativism of postmodernism and its mockery of the possibility of an *international* sociology, she argued for the 'fundamental unicity of Humanity' that, in turn, necessitates 'a single discipline' for 'a single world' (1991: 131; quoted in Adesina 2002: 94). While Akiwowo's project could be seen to be at odds with such an understanding, Archer, however, incorporated his work into her vision. She suggested that the import of his 'pioneering work' is in its demonstration 'that people do think much the same the world over' and the evidence for this is his ability to teach and do 'sociology in the vernacular' by elaborating 'oral Yoruba equivalents for Western socio-logical concepts' (1991: 143). The importance of Akiwowo's 'pioneering work' for Archer, then, is in its confirmation of what was already known and its translation of the dominant paradigm into a 'vernacular' sociology.

Archer's 'Sociology for One World' is a global sociology based on Western sociological concepts where the only space given to other voices is in their translation of these concepts into local idioms. Never mind that these 'local idioms' and 'vernaculars' are to other people what 'English' is to Archer (see Adesina 2002: 110 fn 7). As Adesina argues, Archer's evocation of a 'single humanity' is one that 'assumes its "unicity" by denying a voice to the non-Western voices. (And the non-dominant voices in the West, as well)' (2002: 94). There is little, as far as Archer is concerned, to be learned by the West from sociologists

make what is foreign more relevant to local conditions and needs', that is, to domesticate and then, over time, change the disciplines (1988: 177). Although, even as he himself acknowledged, this recommendation preserved the relationship of intellectual dependency that was otherwise under critique. Dependency theory did, however, provoke a more profound challenge to the intellectual formation of the social sciences in the Latin American debates. As Mignolo suggests, the early work of the Colombian sociologist, Orlando Fals Borda, used dependency theory to argue not just for a 'project in the social sciences for the liberation of the Third World; rather, it concerned also a project of intellectual liberation from the social sciences' (Mignolo 2002: 65). Fals Borda's argument was that dependency was not only economic and political, but also intellectual and that this 'epistemic dependence' had to be recognized and addressed as part of any broader address of relations of dominance. This would involve not simply using 'Western' knowledge until such a time as an 'indigenous' critique could be developed, as suggested by Gareau above. But, rather, recognizing that knowledge is produced in particular historical and cultural conditions and is not straightforwardly transferrable to other contexts. As such, as Fals Borda writes, it is important and necessary to develop local 'theoretical models to interpret correctly and coherently the problems of our society' (1980: 163). In this, he was followed by scholars such as Enrique Dussel arguing also for a philosophy of liberation from the south, where the south was not simply a geographic location, but an epistemological position (see Mignolo 2002). In Dussel's own words, the philosophy of liberation was 'a critical philosophy self-critically localised in the periphery, within subaltern groups' (2008: 340). This did not mean that other philosophical traditions were not engaged with, but that this engagement was oriented to taking what was useful in terms of contributing 'to a justification of the praxis of liberation' (Dussel 2008: 342).

The presumed necessity of holding onto the philosophical and humanist traditions of 'European' social science at the same time as being sensitive to local conditions was also posited by Roberto Briceño-León and Heinz R. Sonntag (1997b) in their Introduction to the ISA's regional volume on Latin American Sociology. Within this volume, Quijano (1997) argues for a form of cultural subversion and 're-originalization' in the patterns and production of social-scientific knowledge. In the absence of subversion, he suggests, 'there is no way to produce any alternative', but if that subversion is not successful then 'its products, statements and virtualities are most likely to be co-opted and assimilated by the dominant pattern' (1997: 33). Any meaningful decolonization of knowledge, he argues, has to occur in the broader context of the social, political and economic decolonization and democratization of society. In this way, Quijano directly links the material and epistemic challenges facing 'decolonial' thinking. This is elaborated further in his development of the coloniality-modernity paradigm together with Walter Mignolo and María Lugones. This is the subject of a subsequent chapter and will be discussed at greater length there. For now, these themes of dependence and subversion are precisely what scholars such as Syed Hussein Alatas had also been arguing for and this chapter will go on to discuss the development of 'alternative' or 'autonomous' approaches to global sociology in East Asia.

III

Syed Hussein Alatas, a prominent Malaysian sociologist, independently arrived at similar themes and developed them in the 1960s and 1970s with his critique of 'the captive mind'. He argued against the unthinking assimilation of Western concepts and categories by Third World scholars and urged them to free themselves from the twin perils of intellectual domination by, and subservience to, Western social science. He developed this idea initially in the context of development studies, but then broadened his argument to call for 'intellectual emancipation' more generally (Alatas, S. H. 1979, 2000). Alongside outlining 'the problem of the captive mind', S. H. Alatas (1979) advocated the establishment of autonomous sociological traditions. His key proposal was that scholars in other parts of the world needed to draw on their pre-colonial civilizational heritage in order to develop autochthonous concepts and traditions which could then be brought into dialogue with Western ones, thereby beginning the process of a proper universalization, or globalization, of social science, created through dialogue as an alternative to the simple adoption of Western traditions, masquerading as sociology as such. As should be clear, the development of autonomous traditions was not to be based on a *rejection* of Western paradigms or concepts but, rather, is seen to involve a process of selectivity based on an assessment of the usefulness of the paradigms or concepts in question. An autonomous tradition, for S. H. Alatas, is based on 'genuine creative assimilation from abroad' of 'whatever is necessary for progress' together with drawing as much as possible from one's own traditions (2000: 27).

In putting forward this alternative argument for the establishment of an autonomous social science tradition, S. H. Alatas (2002, 2006) was keen to distinguish it from the earlier arguments for indigenization. He argued that the two approaches should not be confused and that reflecting on the differences between them was no 'mere wrangling on terminology' but rather highlighted serious deficiencies with the indigenization paradigm (Alatas, S. H. 2002: 155). The domain of the latter was understood to be that of 'customs, usages, plants, animals, climate and food habits', that is, the domain of the 'relative and particular', rather than the 'general and universal', which was instead associated with Western social science and the autonomous traditions approach (Alatas, S. H. 2002: 155). As such, according to S. H. Alatas, indigenization could not facilitate the development of the social sciences, as its focus was on 'fitting the entity [Western social science] into a pre-existing mould' rather than breaking away 'from the existing scheme of things' to create something new (2002: 155, 156). The implicit criticism here is twofold. First, that the project of indigenization accepted Western social science wholesale and simply adapted it to fit with local conditions. There was deemed to be no break with the dominant Western paradigm or any attempt to create a new tradition distinct from that paradigm. Instead, indigenization was seen as part of the process of 'imitative' thinking that indicated a failure to decolonize knowledge and was presented as a mere variation of Western social science. Second, that indigenization remained locked within a particularistic, ethnographic frame that did not seek to create 'universal' knowledge. Instead, it is presented as a 'distortion', or even 'mutilation', of the social-scientific endeavour (Alatas, S. H. 2006: 11). While these criticisms are asserted, they are not demonstrated, and the differences as they are presented appear to rest more on a division between tropes of indigeneity or nativism, on the one hand, and civilization on the other (see also Alatas, S. F. 2001).

The focus on a civilizational context, for the development of autonomous traditions of sociology, aligns this approach with that espoused by theorists of multiple modernities. In both approaches, the Western social-scientific tradition, linked to modernity, is given centrality and is regarded, as S. H. Alatas states, as 'the definitive reference point for departure and progress in the development of sociology' in other places (2006: 10). This is primarily a consequence, in his view, of the Western tradition being the first to formalize the collective response of a group of scholars into the discipline of sociology. It is not to suggest, however, that sociological thought could not have emerged independently elsewhere – and, indeed, S. H. Alatas (2006) and S. F. Alatas (2010) point to the earlier sociological insights of scholars such as Ibn Khaldun and Jose Rizal – but that, given the contemporary hegemony of the Western tradition, sociological endeavours in other places have to now take this tradition into account in their own development. Alongside this, as S. F. Alatas argues, autonomous traditions need to be 'informed by local/ regional historical experiences and cultural practices' as well as by alternative 'philosophies, epistemologies, histories, and the arts' (2010: 37); the 'autonomy' of the different traditions, then, rests on studies of historical phenomena believed to be unique to particular areas or societies. In this way, Western social science becomes a reference point for divergence (creativity, as

5

Global Sociology: Multiple, Southern, Provincial?

This chapter continues the discussion of global sociology focusing on the arguments made by scholars based, largely, in Western/northern locations. It looks first at Raewyn Connell's argument for 'southern' theory and Boaventura de Sousa Santos's related arguments against northern epistemology and for a theory from the south. It then goes on to address the work of sociologists Sujata Patel and Michael Burawoy, who have been actively promoting ideas of global sociology and arguing for a 'provincialized' social science.

I

Raewyn Connell (1997, 2007a) is unusual among sociologists for arguing that sociology, at its emergence, had a global sensibility which it then lost in its mid twentieth-century re-organization around a canon and preoccupation with ideas of modernization. She argues that at its inception as a discipline there was no sense within sociology that 'certain texts were discipline-defining "classics" demanding special study' or that there was a particular 'originating event' around which scholarship need cohere (1997: 1514, 1517). The approach was more encyclopaedic than canonical and, she suggests, the research focus of the early sociologists was organized around the theme of 'global difference' rather than understandings of modernity (1997: 1515, 1516–17). Their understanding of 'global difference', Connell continues, came about as a consequence of 'the process of economic and colonial expansion' and thus was a concept bequeathed by empire, rather than 'invented' by those sociologists (1997: 1519). As such, Connell suggests that sociology needs to be understood as shaped by imperialism and as embodying 'a cultural response to the colonized world' (1997: 1519). It is this global sensibility, she argues, that then gets lost and requires recovery. While there may be some truth in Connell's arguments, there are also a number of unresolved issues.

The focus of early sociologists on the difference of 'primitive' societies and the traditions of 'others' was less as an end in itself, as Connell herself admits, and more a demonstration of the difference of these societies from their own societies, which were understood as modern. Thus, it could be argued that their articulation of 'global difference' was precisely an attempt to understand the modernity of their own societies and, usually, the failure of others 'to modernize' even if this wasn't the language explicitly used. In this way, the early sociologists were as interested in ideas of modernity and, indeed, in differentiating between the modern and the traditional, as were the sociologists who came later. Further, understanding 'global difference' as a cultural response to colonization does not indicate a comprehension of the ways in which colonialism was implicated in 'metropole' societies, it simply indicates an awareness of difference between them. This, I would suggest, is not sufficient.

The 'global' in the work of these sociologists was simply the provider of resources for the development of their own understandings of themselves; there was little sense of the global being understood as a world-lived-in-common or the global as the condition for the developments they were witnessing. Instead, the global was a bifurcated world of the modern and the traditional where the dominant explanation for the divide was located in processes internal to the societies developing. The impact of imperialism and colonialism on the creation and maintenance of this divide was little regarded. This effacement was furthered in the 1960s shift from a concern with marking difference 'out there', between modern and traditional societies, to examining the sum, she is sensitive both to the politics of knowledge production in different locations and across and between those locations.

Patel's (2014b) position is double-edged. She argues for the necessity of the global north to provincialize its knowledge and, at the same time, for the global south to build its own networks of endogenous (not indigenous) knowledges. She suggests that while the knowledge of the global south is already provincialized within nationalist frames, these nationalist frames must nonetheless be further decolonized. 'If social sciences of the Atlantic region promoted Eurocentrism,' she argues, 'those of newly independent countries valorized the nation and the state; the visions of its elite became the frames of doing social sciences' (2014b: 44). Further decolonizing these nationalist frames would involve engaging seriously with social movements and acknowledging the many other sites for knowledge production that exist outside the institutional hierarchies of the university. Patel acknowledges that her approach is methodologically nationalist, but argues that methodological nationalism has different implications depending on its location (see also Falola 2005). In formerly colonized countries, developing a specifically nationalist social science was part of the broader project to rebuild indigenous knowledges and traditions after the devastating effects of colonization, both politically and epistemologically. As such, according to Patel (2014a), while methodological nationalism in the global north can be seen to be embedded in a theory of colonial modernity; in the global south it was located in a contestation of colonial modernity and a desire to establish understandings of its own histories of modernity.

In arguing for the importance of recognizing the particularity of other (national) traditions in the face of universalizing processes originating in Europe and the US, Patel's primary argument is for sociologists to acquaint themselves 'with different ways to do sociology across the world' and 'to foster institutionalised dialogue' across different traditions (2010b: 17). With this, she is arguing for the need to compare contextually and to keep ourselves alert to differences, rather than similarities, when doing comparative work. And this, she suggests, is only possible if we also keep open the processes of the production, distribution and consumption of knowledge across all levels – local, national and international. Part of her critique, then, is also a critique of the international institutional structures that continue to privilege knowledge from particular parts of the world, over knowledge from other parts. Patel (2014b) suggests that the uneven distribution of resources and of sites of institutional academic power, such as journal and book publishing, determine the international standards against which other traditions, and academics, of social science are judged. These differential conditions further constrain the possibilities for a truly global sociology, either intellectually or practically, to the extent that they reproduce long-standing (colonial) hierarchies and privileges. Patel's arguments, then, engage both with the intellectual problems of thinking social science globally as well as addressing the global institutional conditions that, in part at least, shape and determine it.

IV

Burawoy's conceptualization of global sociology, in turn, begins with a critique of the project led by Wallerstein to 'open' the social sciences (discussed in an earlier chapter). He suggests that Wallerstein's solution to the contradictions of the nineteenth-century paradigm of the social sciences is more an Olympian reconstruction of them than an address of their deficiencies. In particular, Burawoy points to Wallerstein's concern with developing an alternative 'unitary system' that transcends both disciplines and history as another form of 'unelaborated universalism' (2005b: 510). Further, in not addressing the material inequalities in the production of sociology in different locations, Burawoy suggests that Wallerstein simply presents 'a unity of the already powerful' (2010b: 64). In contrast, Burawoy argues for bursting 'the bubble of disinterested knowledge' and grounding the social sciences 'in their particularity and their specific context of production' (2005b: 508–9).

V

This chapter and the previous one have perhaps been unusual in considering the development of sociological arguments in the context of disciplinary organizations such as the ISA. Given that the expansion of higher education in many locations has been facilitated by nation state projects and the latter have been most concerned with building education for employment and national citizenship, it is perhaps not surprising that discussions of the discipline should fall so readily into national expressions.[7] 'Civil society' is the sociological concept that is most oriented to national contexts and, in consequence, it is not surprising that the association of sociology with civil society should reinforce the problem of methodological nationalism. However, it is disappointing that the explicit form of global sociology that has been developed in the dialogues generated by the ISA should remain so embedded in a debate between local traditions and (European) universalism (as expressed by Archer (1991) and Sztompka (2011)).

Global social relations have rarely been civil – expressions of voluntary associative activities – in the sense attributed to the civil societies of most sociological analysis. Transnational political domination has been sustained by force and membership in political communities stratified by the racial hierarchies established through colonialism and empire. Global sociology addressed to a global civil society must, at best, be a hope rather than an expression of the relations among current sociologies and the populations they address. The final section of the book now turns to a consideration of the work by theorists who explicitly acknowledge the construction of the global through processes of colonialism and imperialism.

---

[7] See, for example, Singh (1979) and Patel (2010c) on the development of Indian sociology and various chapters in Burawoy, Chang and Hsieh (2010) for developments within other national sociologies.

Part Three

Connected Sociologies

6

Postcolonial and Decolonial Reconstructions

Postcolonial and decolonial arguments have been explicit in their challenge to the insularity of historical narratives and historiographical traditions emanating from Europe. This has been particularly so in the context of demonstrating the parochial character of arguments about the endogenous European origins of modernity in favour of arguments that suggest the necessity of considering the emergence of the modern world in the broader histories of colonialism, empire and enslavement. As postcolonial and decolonial criticisms have become increasingly common, however, proponents of more orthodox views often make minor adjustments and suggest that this is all now very familiar and that, while the critique may once have had cogency, its force now is only in relation to positions that have already been superseded. In this way, the approaches discussed in the earlier chapters, such as multiple modernities, often seek to supplement, or marginally modify, existing approaches in terms of their future application, rather than to transform them. In contrast, my argument is that the postcolonial and decolonial critique has not properly been acknowledged, let alone superseded. Importantly, as I have argued in previous chapters, any transformation of understandings would require a reconstruction 'backwards' of our historical accounts of modernity, as well as 'forwards' in terms of constructing a sociology adequate for our global (postcolonial) age. In this chapter, I examine the traditions of postcolonialism and decolonial thinking and discuss how their radical potential in unsettling and reconstituting standard processes of knowledge production might be drawn upon as part of a larger project for 'connected sociologies'.

The traditions of thought associated with postcolonialism and decoloniality are long-standing and diverse. Postcolonialism emerged as a movement consolidating and developing around the ideas of Edward W. Said, Homi K. Bhabha and Gayatri C. Spivak and drawing inspiration from the political movements for decolonization and the related scholar-activists associated with and central to such struggles. While much work in the area of Postcolonial Studies has directly addressed issues of the material, of the socioeconomic, there has also been a tendency for it to remain firmly in the realm of the cultural. This is no accident, given its intellectual provenance in the humanities more generally and English Literature more specifically. In contrast, the coloniality/modernity school emerged from the work of, among others, the sociologists Aníbal Quijano and María Lugones, and the philosopher and semiotician, Walter D. Mignolo. It was strongly linked to world systems theory from the outset as well as to scholarly work in development and underdevelopment theory and the Frankfurt School critical social theory tradition. More recently, it has sought to draw upon a broader range of theorists and activists from more diverse locations and across a longer time period.

As well as a disciplinary difference, there is also a difference in geographical 'origin' and remit; that is, the geographical locations from where the scholars within the particular fields hail and the geographical focus of their studies. Postcolonialism emerged both as a consequence of the work of diasporic scholars from the Middle East and South Asia and, for the most part, refers back to those locations and their imperial interlocutors (Europe and the West/ North America). Decoloniality similarly emerged from the work of diasporic scholars from South America and, for the most part, refers back to those locations and their imperial interlocutors – again, primarily to Europe although addressing a much longer time frame. Whereas postcolonialism refers primarily to the nineteenth and twentieth centuries, decoloniality starts with the earlier European incursions upon the lands that came to be known as the Americas from the fifteenth century onwards. There has been little work, thus far, bringing together the intellectual and material histories of these fields. This chapter is one contribution to this larger project as well as establishing the theoretical basis for the further elaboration of 'connected sociologies' in the final chapter.

I

Postcolonial Studies emerged as an academic field in the wake of the publication of Edward W. Said's ground-breaking book, *Orientalism* (1995 [1978]). The contours of this field were further shaped by Homi K. Bhabha's collection of essays, *The Location of Culture* (1994), and Gayatri C. Spivak's preface to Derrida's *Of Grammatology* and her oft-cited article, 'Can the Subaltern Speak?' (1998). While this triumvirate of critical literary scholars formed the canonical hub of Postcolonial Studies, they were augmented by many others from across the humanities and social sciences. Alongside the inclusion of scholars associated with the Birmingham Centre for Contemporary Cultural Studies (Hall 1992; Gilroy 1993) and the Subaltern Studies collective (Guha 1982, 1983; Chakrabarty 2000), Postcolonial Studies was also defined by its retrospective inclusion of earlier scholar-activists such as Frantz Fanon (1963, 1967 [1952]), Albert Memmi (1965 [1957]), and Aimé Césaire (1972 [1955]). There are a number of excellent works outlining and summarizing the field as a whole (see, for example, Gandhi 1998; Loomba 2005; Mongia 2000) and it is not my intention to provide a comprehensive overview here, given the range of contributions across the humanities and social sciences. Instead, I wish simply to pick up on some of the defining debates that have been significant in my articulation of postcolonial theory within the social sciences; this is a necessarily selective and incomplete account. While the humanities have engaged extensively with the idea of the postcolonial and with the field of Postcolonial Studies, the social sciences, generally, have been more resistant to rethinking in light of such interventions – whether those of Walter Rodney and Frantz Fanon in the 1960s or those subsequent ones self-consciously defined as postcolonial.

With *Orientalism*, not only did Said present a thorough-going critique of the arcane discipline of Oriental Studies, but he opened up the question of the production of knowledge from a global perspective. While he was not the first to address such a question, his positioning of it in the context of interrogating the Orient/Occident divide was novel. He unsettled the terrain of any argument concerned with the 'universal' by demonstrating how the idea of the universal was based both on an analytic bifurcation of the world and an elision of that bifurcation. This double displacement removed the 'other' *from* the production of an effective history of modernity. History became the product of the West in its actions upon others. At the same time, it displaced those actions in the idea that modernity was endogenous to the West and therefore removed the very question of the 'other' *in* history. In so doing, it also naturalized and justified the West's material domination of the 'other' and in this way suggested the complicity between Orientalism as scholarly discourse and as imperial institution. It was no accident then, as Said suggests, that the movements for decolonization from the early twentieth century onwards should provoke a fundamental crisis within Orientalist thought; a crisis that fractures the complacent rendering of the 'other' as passive and docile and which challenges the assumptive conceptual framework underpinning such depictions. These defining arguments have been central to my research.

The errors committed by the Orientalists, Said argues, were twofold: first, they got things wrong because there was no Orient to depict; second, the Orient they described was a misrepresentation. Critics of Said have suggested that making such an argument is contradictory as there can be no misrepresentation of something that does not exist (MacKenzie 1995; Irwin 2007). While the argument is complex, it is not unfathomable. As Said argues, 'The Orient that appears in Orientalism … is a system of representations framed by a whole set of forces that brought the Orient into Western learning, Western consciousness, and later, Western empire' (1995 [1978]: 202–3). In setting up the Orient as the 'other' of the West, Orientalists cumulatively (along with other scholars) created something in conceptual terms that did not pre-exist its categorization. This was done by separating out conceptually parts of the world which were historically and empirically interconnected, resulting in two ideal types devoid of adequate material referents: the universal, unexamined West which was elided with the notion of world history, and the particular, stagnant Orient which, as a temporally and spatially distinct entity, provided its counterpart. Depictions of this Orient then served to establish the truth of the conceptual categories rather than standing as an adequate representation of what was being 'observed'. Orientalists misrepresented the Orient, in part, because what they were looking at was filtered through the cumulative discourse which already suggested what there was to see – two disparate, unconnected entities, with characteristics specific to each. In this way, they both created the Orient, as a general category, and misrepresented what was then observed.

With this, Said is not suggesting that there is a real or true Orient that could have been known, but rather is provoking us to consider how what we know is itself framed as knowledge through particular systems of representation and the practices of colonial governance based upon them. He further pushes us to question the adequacy of those systems not in terms of their supposed fidelity to what is observed, but in terms of a broader ethical project. The issue is less that Orientalists got things wrong when they could have got them right and more that their interpretations were allied to and reinforced particular world views which justified forms of colonial governance and domination. The fundamental issue is to address the specific sets of connections that have been made from particular instances and to argue that other interconnections can also be made. Addressing other interconnections would provide an understanding of the world, one that would be no less interpretive, but more adequate in explaining the conditions of events in their own terms and in relation to wider interconnections. This would also embrace an ethical position that acknowledges the value of human beings and human experience in global context. Orientalism, Said argues, both failed to identify *with* human experience, or to see it *as* human experience (1995: 328). The ethical impetus behind the best of work within Postcolonial Studies moves us in the other direction.

The central thesis of Said's work rests on an understanding of human identity, whether individual or collective, as constructed, that is, 'constantly being made and unmade' (1995: 333). Fundamental to this is the 'idea of rethinking and re-formulating historical experiences which had once been based on the geographical separation of peoples and cultures' and basing them instead on notions of intertwined histories and overlapping territories (1995: 353; see also, 1994). Said's work is characterized through its crossing of presupposed boundaries even as it abjures the existence of those boundaries and it takes seriously the question of how one *represents* other cultures at the same time as questioning what *another* culture is (Said 1995: 325). In responding to such questions, Said urges methodological caution in that he suggests we need to submit our methods to critical scrutiny and be vigilant in ensuring that our work remains responsive to the material issues with which it engages. His primary conclusion for us, as scholars and academics engaged with the world, is to guard against indifference in our scholarship. We need to keep in mind, Said concludes, that 'human history is made by human beings. Since the struggle for control over territory is part of that history, so too is the struggle over historical and social meaning' (1995: 331).

It is this insight, perhaps above all others, that has become central to the broader project of Postcolonial Studies and is one that is developed at length within the work of Homi Bhabha. The publication of Bhabha's book, *The Location of Culture*, in 1994 brought together a series of ground-breaking essays published in a variety of journals over the previous decade. These essays cover a number of themes, but coalesce around a dual engagement with social ethics and subject formation on the one hand, and (the representation of) contemporary inequalities and their historical conditions, on the other – as well, of course, as the relationships between these aspects. This is perhaps best captured in Bhabha's words that 'we must not merely change the *narratives* of our histories, but transform our sense of what it means to live' (1994: 256).

Postcolonial theory, according to Bhabha, is no longer (if it ever was) simply about the establishment of separatist trajectories or parallel interpretations, but should be seen instead as 'an attempt to interrupt the Western discourses of modernity through ... displacing, inter-rogative subaltern or postslavery narratives and the critical-theoretical perspectives they engender' (1994: 199). The issue is more about re-inscribing 'other' cultural traditions into narratives of modernity and thus transforming those narratives – both in historical terms and theoretical ones – rather than simply renaming or re-evaluating the content of these other 'inheritances'. Modernity, as Bhabha elaborates, 'is not located, a priori, in the passive fact of an epochal event or idea ... but has to be negotiated *within* the "enunciative" present of the discourse' (1994: 201); that is, the meaning of modernity does not derive from a foundational event in the past, but from its continual contestation in the present. This negotiation calls into question both the conditions with which modernity is typically associated and the agents that lay claim to it. In other words, there is no essence to the event or actors of history that can be authentically captured after the event – history is the spectacle created through distance and through the displacement that exists between the event and the spectators. In naming oneself, as Bhabha suggests, one moves from the periphery to the centre and in the process transforms the understanding of 'modernity' from which and about which one speaks.

For Bhabha, then, there is no singular event of modernity and there are no moderns (that is, those who have lived through modernity); rather, modernity 'is about the historical construction of a specific position of historical enunciation and address' (201–2) and much can be learnt through examining the spatial contours given by theorists to the time of modernity. The insistent location of modernity in the French and industrial revolutions, for example, reveals the 'eurocen-tricity of Foucault's theory of cultural difference' (Bhabha 1994: 202);

a eurocentricity that is made more apparent when we address the case of Haiti, among others (see Bhambra 2007 for discussion). By interrupting the passage of modernity, the assumed temporal action of modernity, what is revealed is the particular staging of modernity. By bearing witness to different pasts one is not a passive observer but is able to turn from interrogating the past to initiating new dialogues about that past and thus bringing into being new histories and from those new histories, new presents and new futures. Postcolonial critical discourse at its best, Bhabha suggests, 'contests modernity through the establishment of other historical sites, other forms of enunciation' (1994: 254) and, in doing so, rearticulates understandings of modernity and the political possibilities associated with it. Bhabha demonstrates this process himself through his reading of Frantz Fanon's (1967 [1953]) *Black Skin, White Masks'.*

In this book, Fanon interrogates the limits of ideas of the universal as commonly presented within concepts such as 'Man' in European social and political thought. He does this by demonstrating the historicity of such concepts, that is, their location within a particular history, and by refusing to be limited by that history in his articulation (and expansion) of the ideas expressed within and by the concept. Bhabha (1994) suggests that the theoretical manoeuvre made by Fanon occurs in the following way. First, Fanon performs the desire of the colonized to be identified as Man, that is, as universal. The response of (white) Men to him (a black man) suggests that he is not Man like them *and* that they have the right (power) to determine who is to count as Man. As a consequence of his racial and cultural differences, Fanon is interpellated as not-yet Man. This temporal distortion is effected by colonialism and described as 'belatedness': the Black Man is not-yet Man, he is Black Man. It is this inscription of a temporal disjuncture within a racialized categorization, itself presented as the 'other side' of the universal concept of Man that Fanon uses to dismantle the structure of power and identity that is established in such a move (Bhabha 1994: 194). By rejecting the notion of 'belatedness', of not-yet being in/of (modern) time, Fanon rejects the temporal disjuncture which legitimizes his particular claim to the universal in the terms posited by European social and political thought; that is, he rejects the idea that his claim to the universal can only be a deferred one, one that is not-yet possible. In so doing, he also rejects 'the *framing* of the white man as universal, normative' (Bhabha 1994: 195) and exposes the hidden structures of this tradition which maintain exclusion and hierarchy in the name of the universal.

Fanon's refusal of the position of the subaltern, of the 'other side' of the universal, is a refusal also of the deferral necessary to a dialectical conception of history based on the idea of an emergence, in the future, of an equitable universality. He reconceptualizes the temporality of modernity in terms that recognize the coevality of peoples and cultures and provokes us to think of the universal from beyond its parochial articulations in European social and political thought. As Bhabha (1994: 196) argues, the move made by Fanon is not a postmodern move advocating the plurality of cultures and viewpoints, but rather is one that illustrates the social contradictions and cultural differences that constitute the disjunctive space of modernity and one that then calls for its re-articulation along egalitarian lines. Postmodern perspectives, Bhabha suggests, increasingly narrativize the question of social ethics and subject formations (1994: 197); that is, 'what is considered to be the essential gesture of Western modernity [is] an 'ethics of self-construction"' (1994: 197). Social construction does not itself imply a form of universalism. Indeed, it frequently implies the opposite. However, insofar as social construction also constructs the 'other' then it is, as Bhabha suggests, 'ethnocentric in its construction of cultural 'difference"' (1994: 197). We create ourselves at the same time as creating 'others', the non-moderns. Postcolonial scholarship, as has been discussed, has been integral to the exercise of opening out and questioning the implied assumptions of the dominant discourses by way of which we attempt to make sense of the worlds we inhabit. It has further provided the basis from which to reclaim, as Spivak argues, 'a series of regulative political concepts, the *supposedly* authoritative narrative of whose production was written elsewhere' (1990: 225). The task, following Spivak, is less about the uncovering of philosophical ground than in 'reversing, displacing, and seizing the apparatus of value-coding' itself (1990: 228); thus, I would suggest, accepting the possibility, in times of the postcolonial, of a critical realignment of colonial power and knowledge through what I set out in the conclusion as a methodology of 'connected sociologies'.

Of the three postcolonial theorists addressed here, Gayatri C. Spivak has probably the most fractious relationship with the field. She first came to international renown with her 1976 translation of Jacques Derrida's *Of Grammatology* and, more specifically, with her translator's preface to the volume. Her reputation was consolidated with the publication, a decade later, of her essay, 'Can the Subaltern Speak?' (1988), and her work, more generally, contributed to the increasing significance given to feminist and Derridean themes within Postcolonial Studies. In this section, I focus on this latter essay and look in particular at the way in which Spivak addresses Western efforts to problematize the subject and, in the process, questions how the Third World subject is represented in Western discourse.

In 'Can the Subaltern Speak?', Spivak offers an analysis of the relationship between Western discourses and the possibility of speaking of (or for) the subaltern (woman). She assesses the intellectual and political contributions of French post-structuralist theory and finds it wanting in terms of its failures in addressing the implications of imperialism in discussions of power and epistemic violence more generally. She suggests that for all that is good and innovative in what has been written there is still a problem to the extent that the question of ideology is ignored, as is the post-structuralist theorist's own implication in intellectual and economic history. To work with 'a self-contained version of the West', she argues, 'is to ignore its production by the imperialist project' (1988: 289). This is not to suggest that the history of imperialism is the only history of the West, but to address more explicitly the question of how what is currently dominant and hegemonic came to be so. The silence of scholars such as Deleuze and Foucault on the (epistemic) violence of imperialism would matter less, she suggests, if they did not choose to speak on Third World issues. Their silence is contrasted with Derrida's position, which sees the European subject's tendency to constitute the other as marginal, as one of the central problems of European philosophy that requires address (1988: 292).

Spivak situates her critique of post-structuralism – and, by implication, postmodernism more generally – in an address of the schematic opposition between interest and desire that is established in even the most critical forms of thought; where 'interest' constitutes the 'external' basis for the formation of subjects (structuralism) and 'desire' the subject's internal mode of self-formation (post-structuralism/ modernism). She suggests that while this opposition is problematic in itself, it is nonetheless more important to attend to the historical construction of representation through 'interest' than try to rethink the individual through concepts such as power and desire (1988: 279). This latter move, she continues, allows for the sort of slippage that results in the Subject of Europe being reinscribed as the 'sun' around which all else revolves. By ignoring the international division of labour, which constitutes the unacknowledged ground upon which theory is articulated, the 'other' is uniformly homogenized as other at the same time as the diversity of 'us' is valorized. Instead, Spivak argues for an 'unlearning' that would involve recognition of the ideological formation of the subject as an object of investigation (1988: 296). Too often, she argues, European philosophers have masqueraded as absent non-representers who seemingly allow, unproblematically, the oppressed to speak for themselves without considering the economic and intellectual privilege this involves (1988: 292, 293). By attending to the ways in which we, particularly as intellectuals, are formed by interests would enable us to begin to see the political implications of our own claims to transparency, particularly in our relations to others (1988: 279). This would further involve recognition of the hidden frames of thought within which those others are slotted (see also Trouillot 1991).

The question of voice is central to Spivak's essay and is developed more fully in the concluding sections of it. She argues that to render the thinking subject transparent is to efface the relentless recognition of the 'other' by assimilation and that what is needed is to develop work on the mechanics of the constitution of others; rather than simply to invoke their authenticity (1988: 294). As she argues in her critique of the early project of Subaltern Studies, it is necessary to recognize the heterogeneity of the colonized subaltern subject and, at the same time, guard against the privileging of subaltern consciousness; not to do so is to fall into a project of a reifying essentialism and taxonomy (1988: 284). The issue, for Spivak, is less the subjective experience of oppression, or the identity claims of the subject, and more understanding (and uncovering) the mechanisms and structures of domination. 'It is the slippage', as she argues, 'between rendering visible the mechanism and rendering vocal the subject' that is problematic (1988: 285). While her conclusion to this essay has often been understood as responding in the negative to the question posed in the title, I would suggest that the force of Spivak's argument is somewhat different. She suggests that the extent to which the subaltern is destined to remain mute is a consequence of mistranslations emerging from the relations of power involved in the colonial encounter and their reinscription into the dominant modes of knowledge production. In a similar fashion to Bhabha, then, the force of the critique from subalterneity is part of the process of reconfiguring the subaltern/power dichotomy in order to bring about a different present within which we speak (and listen).

The field of Postcolonial Studies, as configured by the three scholars discussed here, is strongly animated by the politics of decolonization beyond the academy, while their theoretical critiques are oriented to the processes of knowledge production largely within the academy. The particular academic battlefields are different for each, as illustrated above, but they dovetail into a critique that is greater than the sum of its individual parts. I now wish to delineate the contours of the related field of coloniality/modernity. While Postcolonial Studies as a field retrospectively ordered the individual intellectual contributions of scholars, the modernity/coloniality project was a more planned endeavour, partly in response to the success of postcolonialism within the academy. This research collective, organized by Walter Mignolo and Arturo Escobar, brought together scholars of Latin American/ European origin working in universities in the US and Latin America and interested in ideas of dependency theory, colonialism, gender and critical theory (see Mignolo 2007a, 2007b). It built on the earlier work of scholars such as Enrique Dussel and Aníbal Quijano and sought, in particular, to examine the relationship between the Frankfurt School version of critical theory and the emerging paradigm of coloniality/modernity; and, indeed, decolonial thinking is understood 'as a particular kind of critical theory' (Mignolo 2007a: 155). In the following section, I discuss this paradigm as articulated by its most prominent advocates: Aníbal Quijano, María Lugones and Walter Mignolo.

II

The theoretical distinction, modernity/coloniality, was first articulated by Aníbal Quijano and published in the late eighties and early nineties as 'Colonialidad y modernidad-racionalidad'. In this article, reprinted in English in the journal *Cultural Studies* in 2007, he argues that with the conquest of the lands that we now call Latin America 'began the constitution of a new world order, culminating, five hundred years later, in a global power covering the whole planet' (2007: 168). This coloniality of power, expressed through political and economic spheres, Quijano continues, was strongly associated with a coloniality of knowledge (or of imagination), articulated as modernity/rationality. This was predicated on a belief that knowledge, in a similar way to property, ought to be considered 'as a relation between one individual and something else' (2007: 173), not as an intersubjective relation for the purpose of something. The individuated form of knowledge production has as its correlate the 'radical absence of the "other"' and a denial of 'the idea of the social totality' (2007: 173). This enables

Europeans, both individually and collectively, to affirm their sense of self at the same time as making invisible the colonial order that provides the context for their 'self'-realization. As Quijano states, the emergence of the idea of Europe is an admission of identity in that it emerges through a process of differentiation *from* other cultures. Yet there is little reflection within European social and political thought on how those other cultures constitute the ground of European self-realization (in both senses). Rather, most discussions of Europe are oriented towards endogenous explanations of who Europeans are and what Europe is. Against this dominant conception, Quijano argues that the modernity that Europe takes as the context for its own being is, in fact, so deeply imbricated in the structures of European colonial domination over the rest of the world that it is impossible to separate the two: hence, modernity/coloniality.

Quijano further points to the contradiction between the disavowal of the idea of totality within European thought and its realization through 'undesirable political practices' based on an ideology of 'the total rationalisation of society' (2007: 176). While this particular political practice of totality within Europe may have tainted the very idea of social totality for many thinkers, Quijano argues that it is not necessary to reject the whole idea but, rather, just that aspect elaborated within the European modernity/coloniality paradigm. Beyond Europe, he continues, most cultures work with a perspective of totality in knowledge that 'includes the acknowledgement of the heterogeneity of all reality … and therefore of the social' (2007: 177). Within such conceptions, difference is not understood in hierarchical terms or in terms expressing superiority or inferiority; instead, 'historical-cultural heterogeneity implies the co-presence and the articulation of diverse historical "logic[s]"' (2007: 177). This understanding enables critique of the European paradigm of modernity/coloniality to be more than 'a simple negation of all its categories' and aim instead for a more thorough-going process of epistemological decolonization that, as Quijano suggests, will 'clear the way for new intercultural communication … as the basis of another rationality which may legitimately pretend to some universality' (2007: 177). Paraphrasing Quijano (2007): there is nothing more irrational than continuing to believe that the idea of universality as articulated by a particular people, and even specified as *Western* rationality, could continue to be understood as universal.

Quijano's understanding of the coloniality of power has had much resonance within academic debates oriented to understanding modernity and colonialism as co-constitutive, particularly within the Latin American and Caribbean contexts (see, for example, Maldonado-Torres 2007; Vázquez 2011; Walsh 2002; Wynter 2003). Maldonado-Torres, for example, transforms the idea of the coloniality of power to the 'coloniality of Being' and uses this 'to thematize the question of the effects of coloniality in lived experience' (2007: 242). He develops this argument through a consideration of European philosophy and, in particular, its limits in relation to theorizing the reality of the colonial world and its production of colonial subjects as invisible and dehumanized. The key issue for Maldonado-Torres is that the supposedly unfinished (democratic) project of modernity, as theorized by Habermas, ought actually to be understood as 'the unfinished project of decolonisation' (2007: 263). Wynter similarly engages with European philosophy in order to unsettle its institution of 'a new principle of nonhomogeneity' consolidated around the 'Color (cum Colonial) Line' (2003: 322). She dissects the philosophical moves made within European thought to elide biocentric descriptive statements with descriptive statements, and argues instead for a new science of the Word, following Césaire, that would be the basis of producing knowledge about our uniquely human domain and 'the urgent problems that beleaguer humankind' (2003: 328); something that the natural sciences have been unable or unwilling to do.

Beyond an engagement with Quijano's idea of the coloniality of power, what these different contributions share is, as Walsh puts it, an understanding that the 'geohistorical colonial difference created by the coloniality of power' has not only subalternized 'ethnic-racial groups but also their knowledge' (2002: 62); and it is to the recovery and re-articulation of that knowledge that these scholars and activists orient their academic work. Vázquez builds on this, by arguing for wider recognition of the way in which social struggles challenge and define 'the oppressive grammars of power' (2010: 41). In this way, he suggests, the conceptual vocabularies of the academy can be displaced and re-signified with meanings that emerge from 'political practices, alternative forms of justice, other ways of living' (2010: 41). As discussed earlier, however, in relation to Postcolonial Studies, my intention here is not to survey the full extent of the research programme of modernity/coloniality, but rather to point to the key debates and theoretical insights that have been most significant for me in the development of this particular research project. In this section, then, I will limit my fuller discussion first to María Lugones' particular interpretation of the coloniality of power in the context of making an argument for a decolonial feminism, before addressing Walter Mignolo's sustained engagement and development of this term.

Lugones builds on Quijano's coloniality of power by arguing for modernity/coloniality to be understood as simultaneously shaped through specific articulations of race, gender and sexuality. This is not to provide a raced or gendered (alternative) *reading* of the paradigm of modernity/coloniality, but rather to re-read modernity/ coloniality from a consciousness of race, gender and sexuality *and* to examine the emergence and development of those categories within this context. Lugones argues that not only did colonization invent the colonized, it also disrupted the social patterns, gender relations and cosmological understandings of the communities and societies it invaded. In doing so, it rearticulated particular European understandings of gender and sex from a bifurcation between male and female to a racialized under-standing of the same embedded within a logic of colonial difference. This further overlay and sought to erase the varied conceptualizations of gender, sex and sexuality that pre-existed the European colonial/ modern gender system. This system organizes the world into homoge-neous, separable categories arranged through hierarchical dichotomies and categorial logics which, in the process, erase colonized women from most areas of social life. As Lugones argues, for example, to suggest that 'woman' and 'black' are homogeneous, separable categories, 'then their intersection shows us the absence of black women rather than their presence' (2010: 742).

This is an absence or an erasure that is exacerbated by the failure of decolonial theorists to take seriously the intersection of race, gender and sexuality with the modernity/coloniality paradigm. Lugones suggests that the contemporary global system of power is affirmed by any 'transnational intellectual and practical work that ignores the imbrication of the coloniality of power and the colonial/modern gender system' (2007: 188). She points to the important linkages between the works of decolonial scholars and feminist scholars of colour – such as Mignolo's borrowing of 'border thinking' from Anzaldua – and argues that resisting the coloniality of gender requires 'seeing the colonial difference' and resisting the 'epistemological habit of erasing it' (2010: 753). Instead, she argues for such resistance to be a 'coalitional starting point' for 'learning about each other' (2010: 753). Lugones, here, builds on and extends the argument made by Quijano (2007), Lorde (2007) and others regarding knowledge as something produced by communities rather than individuals. She argues that given that our ways of living in the world are shared, and so our knowledge of the world is shared, so there is important work to be done in learning from and about each other. Learning from the other does not imply becoming the other or succumbing to the categorical logic of dichotomies that separate and homogenize others. Instead, Lugones argues for the non-reducibility of the multiplicity that emerges in encounters with colonial difference and a plea that '*the fragmented loci can be creatively in coalition*' (2010: 755, italics in original). While Lugones has emphasized the necessary work that must be undertaken by individual scholars and activists within their communities of knowledge to build and maintain coalitions (connections), Mignolo focuses on the interconnections of the narrative histories and epistemologies of such encounters.

The elaboration of the mutual co-constitution of modernity/ coloniality and the extension of the time frame of modernity back to the fifteenth century are two of the key contributions made by Quijano to the reconceptualization of the dominant modes of thought. Both aspects radically challenge standard notions of modernity. The temporal dimension is stretched back from the eighteenth century to the fifteenth century and the spatial dimension is expanded from northern Europe, specifically France and Britain, also to include southern Europe, specifically Spain and Portugal, and Latin America. Acknowledging these shifts establishes colonialism as the precondition for the development of (ideas of) modernity and all subsequent understandings of modernity have to take into account the conditions of its emergence. Mignolo develops Quijano's earlier theoretical work and, in particular, further elaborates his conception of modernity/ coloniality in the context of the work of epistemic decolonization necessary to undo the damage wrought by both modernity and by understanding modernity/coloniality only as modernity. The decolonization of knowledge, he suggests, occurs in acknowledging the sources and geopolitical locations of knowledge while at the same time affirming those modes and practices of knowledge that have been denied by the dominance of particular forms. He is not arguing simply for a geopolitics of location as central to any academic endeavour, but rather a consideration of *what* that geopolitics enables to be known and *how* it is to be known. The key issue for Mignolo is not only that epistemology is not ahistorical, but also, and perhaps more importantly, that epistemology 'has to be geographical in its historicity' (2000: 67). This has also been described by Mignolo (2000) as 'border thinking'.

The border is constituted by the limits of Western philosophy in its failure to address colonial difference, that is, to address or make visible 'the variety of local histories that Western thought ... hid and suppressed' (2000: 66). It is the encounters between a universalist Western philosophy with those other histories, then, that creates the possibilities for 'border thinking' from which concepts, paradigms and histories can be reworked. While 'border thinking' formed a central aspect of Mignolo's early work, it was superseded by his development of the idea of 'de-linking'. This was articulated in the context of the modernity/coloniality paradigm discussed earlier and pointed now to the necessity of an epistemic de-linking from the rhetoric of modernity and a practical de-linking, that is, a struggle to break free, from the logic of coloniality. Whereas previously Mignolo (2000: 91) had argued for a politics of diversality that regionalized the European legacy and located critical thinking in the space of colonial encounters, he now argues for a politics of pluriversality underpinned by an epistemological project of de-linking, subsequently reformulated as the decolonial option (2007, 2011): each will be discussed in turn.

Mignolo's project of 'de-linking' points to the need to change the terms (concepts) as well as the content (histories) of the conversations on modernity/coloniality. He argues for a decolonial epistemic shift that enables the histories and thought of other places to be understood as prior to European incursions and to be used as the basis of developing a connected history of encounters through those incursions. In the process, he argues also for the epistemic de-linking from 'the rhetoric of modernity' to involve rethinking 'the emancipating ideals of modernity in the perspective of coloniality' (2007b: 469). Following Chakrabarty's (2000) earlier phrasing of the concepts and paradigms of the European tradition being indispensable, but inadequate for our understanding of the social world, Mignolo similarly sees these as 'necessary … but highly insufficient' (2007b: 459). This is as a consequence of both Chakrabarty and Mignolo agreeing with the dominant conceptualization of modernity as a phenomenon having emerged in Europe, albeit in the context of an 'other' against which it was (silently) juxtaposed. Therefore, for Mignolo, European understandings of modernity are necessary to the extent that they delineate its emergence and development in Europe, but insufficient to the extent that they fail to address (the relationship of) the 'other' within such processes, or prior to such processes; with the 'other', here, being the initial colonial endeavours of Europeans in Latin America.

The de-linking project, then, seeks 'to de-naturalize concepts and conceptual fields that totalise A [*sic*] reality' (2007b: 459). Mignolo does this, in part, by discussing the significance of Waman Puma de

Ayala, a seventeenth-century indigenous Peruvian writer, who chron-icled the history of Andean civilizations from before the arrival of the Spanish. Mignolo draws on the work of Rolena Adorno, who trans-lated and introduced Waman Puma de Ayala's *Nueva Corónica y Buen Gobierno* (with John V. Murra and Jorge L. Urioste), and concurs with her assessment that bringing this work to wider scholarly attention was 'an act of decolonisation in the forum of historical literary schol-arship' (Adorno cited in Mignolo 2007b: 506 fn 30). He further argues that the *Nueva Corónica* [new chronicle] should not be understood as 'a correction of a Spanish mistake within the same Spanish epistemic logic', but rather, as 'the introduction of a new logic to tell the story' (2007b: 461). This is as a consequence of these chronicles narrating a history of the Andes that locates the Spanish invasion in the context of already existing histories and makes this event one in a series of events as opposed to the foundational event from which history is to be written. Using the example of Waman Puma de Ayala, Mignolo argues for the importance of recovering earlier histories, that is, histories prior to colonization, from which to articulate both alternative possi-bilities of living and modes of resistance to the logics of modernity/coloniality. Shifting the historical frame of significant events from Europe to other parts of the world, and prior to European contact, necessitates 'the re-writing of global history from the perspective and critical consciousness of coloniality' (2007b: 484). This rewriting does not involve the inscription of a new form of universality, but rather, for Mignolo, a new *pluri*versality where 'each local history and its narrative of decolonisation can *connect* through that common experience and use it as the basis for a new common logic of knowing' (2007b: 497).

Pluriversality as a global project, then, is constituted through the decentred connections *between* local histories and oriented *around* 'the decolonial option'. This is the latest theoretical innovation articu-lated by Mignolo (2011) within the broad paradigm of modernity/coloniality and is distinguished from seemingly similar trajectories such as dewesternization as articulated by scholars such as Kishore

Madhubani. Mignolo suggests that while both decoloniality and dewesternization seek to reject the (self-proclaimed) epistemic superiority of the West, dewesternization does not question the capitalist economy with which it is bound, only who leads within it. The decolonial option, on the other hand, starts from the idea that 'the regeneration of life shall prevail over [the] primacy of recycling the production and reproduction of goods' (2011: 121) and aims towards breaking 'the Western code' of modernity/coloniality both epistemologically and materially. Decolonial options, Mignolo continues, enable the building of communal futures different from our pasts; futures that are built around the idea that we 'place human lives and life in general first' (2011: 141). The theoretical shifts in Mignolo's work, from border thinking to de-linking to the decolonial option, are all grounded in the modernity/coloniality paradigm and seek to articulate distinctive positions within the broader debate contesting the dominance of European modes of thought. In the final section of this chapter, I bring together the key contributions of Postcolonial Studies and the modernity/coloniality paradigm to set up how an idea of 'connected sociologies' might emerge from them. This will be discussed more fully in the final chapter.

III

As should be apparent from the preceding discussion, both postcolonialism and decoloniality are developments within the broader politics of knowledge production and both emerge out of political developments contesting the colonial world order established by European empires, albeit in relation to different time periods and different geographical orientations. The key issue to emerge from the work of decolonial scholars is to pull the time horizon of debates on modernity back to the late fifteenth century and extend them southwards to take into account both the activities of southern European countries such as Spain and Portugal, but also the southern half of the continent to be named the Americas. Quijano and then Mignolo after him have also done much to demonstrate the deep imbrications of the development of modernity within coloniality and, in establishing the concept of coloniality, providing us with a way to discuss the more profound realities of colonialism, especially 'after' the event. The colonial matrix of power, that Mignolo argues is the inextricable combination of the rhetoric of modernity (progress, development, growth) and the logic of coloniality (poverty, misery, inequality), has to be central to any discussion of contemporary global inequalities and the historical basis of their emergence.

Lugones extends the arguments of both Quijano and Mignolo to demonstrate how coloniality not only divides the world according to a particular racial logic, but also creates specific understandings of gender that enable the disappearance of the colonial/raced woman from theoretical and political consideration. In this, Lugones is close to Spivak's (1988) considerations in 'Can the Subaltern Speak?' and makes explicit the issue of listening and learning from others in any development away from current dominant structures of knowledge production. In pointing to the importance of coalitions of resistance as well as coalitions of understanding, she highlights the necessary relationship between hierarchies of oppression and the personal politics of knowledge production (where the personal is always understood in terms of the communities within which individuals are located and through which knowledge is produced). All the theorists considered here would argue strongly for such a conception of knowledge production and acknowledge their own debts – intellectual and other – to the communities that sustained and enabled their scholarship; from historical antecedents such as Waman Puma de Ayala (and their translators), to relative contemporaries such as Fanon and Césaire, as well as the academic research communities that develop and take the ideas and initiatives of these scholars beyond their initial conceptualizations.

Said's influence within the academy (and further afield) has been as extensive as it has been diverse. His key theoretical contribution, I would suggest, is the demonstration of how the idea of the universal within European thought is based on a claim to universality at the same time as it elides its own particularity, and how this claim is sustained through the exercise of material power in the world. His argument is not one of immanent critique or the working out of a scholastic position within academic debate, but rather, is focused on exposing the ways in which relations of power underpin both knowledge and the possibilities of its production. Bhabha similarly is committed to the disruption of standard narratives that reinforce particular conceptualizations of power in the name of a broader humanitarian ethos and providing resources for the construction of other narratives. His reading of Fanon, for example, brings to the fore the particular work being done by ideas of the universal within European thought and the deferral that is inserted into those universals when applied to those understood as 'other'. In arguing for the necessity of rearticulating understandings of modernity from other geographical locations and through a consideration of processes of colonization and enslavement, he aligns straightforwardly with scholars of the modernity/coloniality paradigm. Postcolonialism and decoloniality are only made necessary as a consequence of the depredations of colonialism, but in their intellectual resistance to associated forms of epistemological dominance they offer more than simple opposition. They offer, in the words of María Lugones, the possibility of a new geopolitics of knowledge.

7

Sociology for an 'Always-Already' Global Age

The view that modernity and sociology are co-constitutive is routine and common-place within the discipline. The historical narratives underpinning sociological conceptions of modernity have similarly been regarded as uncontested. To the extent that there have been disagreements over them, these have generally been normative, that is, whether modernity should be considered an unalloyed good, or about specific details such as the timing or duration of phases of modernity. Rarely have scholars addressing sociological debates on modernity also addressed the adequacy of the specific histories of modernity articulated within the discipline. In effect, European histories of the Renaissance, the Reformation, the Scientific Revolution and the industrial and French revolutions, have been considered 'world-historical' and, as such, have been utilized as substitutions for 'world history' in a modernity that is claimed to be universal. Any critique of the adequacy of those standard histories as referents for 'world history' has largely come from outside the discipline of sociology. Initially, this was from underdevelopment and dependency theorists and then from theorists of postcolonial and decolonial thought. The central argument of this book is that the neglect of these other histories, which also constitute world history, is an obstacle to a more adequate understanding of the processes that are otherwise seen as central to sociological concerns and that shape its orientations to the future.

In contrast to other approaches within sociology, I have examined the theoretical frameworks and historical narratives at play within standard sociological accounts of the global. I have addressed the ways in which these frameworks and narratives establish the dominant disciplinary and conceptual contours of sociology and have highlighted their limitations. As such, *Connected Sociologies* continues the deconstruction of sociology's narratives of its past, that I began in *Rethinking Modernity*, in order to highlight broader, more extensive connections than are typically addressed and to argue for a reconstruction of sociology on this basis. Drawing upon postcolonial and decolonial arguments, I have suggested that modernity does not itself produce a connected world, but is itself a product of interconnections, or importantly, these interconnections are made up of different forms of domination, appropriation, possession and dispossession that cannot be seen as deriving from a simple logic of capitalist development or expanded market relations.

Sociology, I suggest, arises alongside a self-understanding of a world-historically significant modernity, but the institutions and practices of that modernity are neither self-contained nor adequately expressed within the self-understanding of sociology.

In arguing for an alternative understanding of the emergence of the global within sociology, I am also making an argument for an alternative way of understanding sociology. In this final chapter, I draw out the key themes from the preceding chapters, present the idea of 'connected sociologies' in contrast to the 'ideal type' methodology of comparative historical sociology, and discuss its critical purchase for sociology through an examination of ideas of citizenship associated with sociology's normative claims.

I

The first section of the book addressed a variety of ways in which ideas of the global were understood within different sociological perspectives. Despite their other differences, the one thing that unites the perspectives of modernization theory, underdevelopment and dependency theories, and the approach of multiple modernities is a belief in the idea of the global as constituted through the subsequent interactions of previously separate and independent entities. That is, all three positions read the contemporary world of nation states, or civilizations, back through history and regard globalization (or modernization) as a recent process that brought these entities into meaningful interaction for the first time. Underdevelopment and dependency theories are somewhat different to the extent that they recognize that contemporary inequalities have a historical basis in capitalist relations, but they do not generally connect this to colonialism. The key dissenting voices here are of Fanon (1963) and Rodney (1972) who stipulate the necessity of colonialism as central to the processes of underdevelopment and development, but for the most part, their legacy is ignored in sociological discussions.

There are two common issues here which, I have suggested, require address. First, civilizations are presented as bounded and as having separate and distinct histories and cultures prior to European contact. There is no consideration of the problem of presenting an understanding of civilizations as hermetically sealed phenomena whose only relevant interaction with 'others' is subsequent to the onset of European modernity. The second problem is the way in which European 'interaction' itself is usually euphemized; the processes of colonialism, enslavement, dispossession and appropriation are rendered as mere 'interaction', 'dissemination' or 'spread'. What is at issue here is the adequacy of the historical narratives upon which understandings of European modernity are based and the representation of European impact in terms that evade a proper reckoning. The elision of colonialism and its attendant processes was also a feature of those writers discussed in Chapter 2 – Braudel, Mann and Wallerstein – who had sought a direct address of the historical record in criticism of schematic, functionalist explanations. The historical record to which they had recourse was a selective one and a partial history was made to stand for a universal account. Goldthorpe's (1991) critique of historical sociology, that its practitioners frequently operate with the freedom of a child in a sweetshop, 'picking and mixing' the versions of history that best suit their purposes, appears apt (if his conclusions about the impossibility of an alternative are rather different from my own). What is interesting to note, however, is how limited are the variations in the stories being told. While these scholars *could* choose any histories, they rarely choose those histories which contest the standard racialized narratives confirming the superiority of Europe to which they seem to be committed.

The second section, encompassing Chapters 3 to 5, focused on scholars who sought to rethink sociology and the social sciences more generally in light of the trope of *globalization*. Within both standard perspectives and more critical ones there are a number of similarities. First, there is agreement on globalization as a recent phenomenon or, at the very least, on globalization only becoming significant in the contemporary period. This is associated with a sense that, *now* there is a need to rethink sociology, and the social sciences, for a newly global age. There is general agreement that what they see as the nation state centred sociology of the nineteenth century was both adequate in its time and adequately represented its time. Even though Wallerstein is more critical of the nineteenth-century liberal heritage of the social sciences than most other scholars discussed in this section, he, too, effectively accepts the historical patterns upon which it is based. In any event, the issue for most sociologists discussed here is the trans-formation of sociology for the future, not addressing its problematic relationship to the past. It is only in this context, in thinking about how sociology may need to develop or change to be more adequate for the future that significant differences among the various sociological positions emerge.

On the one hand, there are arguments that sociology contains within it the resources to be different for these different times that we face. Almost through an act of will, or at least through the reinterpretation of existing traditions, sociology, it is suggested by scholars such as Beck, can be transformed now to be responsive to the demands of the global age. An alternative position suggests that this transformation can only come about by taking into account the work of scholars who have previously been excluded, that is, through expanding the canon and pluralizing it. These two modes of modest internal transformation and external pluralism leave intact the history of sociology and the histories central to sociological understandings of modernity. Any transformation is only subsequent to the present; it is not a transformed understanding of how we got to the present. Both modes accept the separatist histories that see globalization and the interconnections they associate with it as only being phenomena of the present and future. In misidentifying the past as unconnected, there is no way in which they can address the inequalities of the present as consequent of shared historical processes. Instead, inequalities are naturalized as the condition of the world, or worlds, within which we find ourselves. Counter-posing the First World to the Third World, for example, without reflecting on how the Third World has been produced by the very same processes that have created the First, is part of this process of naturalization.

Accounting for the contemporary configuration of the world, and addressing the inequalities that we find there, requires taking seriously the understandings of historical processes upon which disciplines are based. The most significant critique has emerged through the bodies of work known as postcolonial and decolonial thought, and discussed at length in Chapter 6. Both take the historical processes of dispossession and colonialism as fundamental to the shaping of the world and to the shaping of the possibilities of knowing the world. The very creation of what we understand the global to be, the interconnections that span the world that enable it to be known empirically as the world, are created in the context of dispossession and appropriation. Dispossession and appropriation are also, then, fundamental to the establishment of how we know the world, and yet in being displaced from our knowledge of the world, disappear from most considerations of it. The establishment of disciplinary knowledge relegates land (dispossession and appropriation) to the realm of anthropology (and geography and development studies) and thereby separates historical injustices from any consideration of justice in 'modern' societies (economics, sociology and political science).

As a consequence, understanding the contemporary configuration of the world requires the dismantling of the disciplinary divides and of the disciplinary edifices constructed upon those divides. This process involves undoing hierarchies and provincializing knowledges, but this is not enough if those knowledges are seen to have been separately constituted and, further, not themselves constituted through connections. Without reconstruction, the radical moment, or movement, of deconstruction will always remain illusory. As Dubois (1935) and Fanon (1963) had recognized previously, it is necessary to build up alternative histories and to establish connections across what has previously been presented as separate. In our present context, it is necessary to create conceptual frameworks that would enable us not just to think sociology (and other social sciences) differently, but also to do it (and them) differently. To think sociology differently is to take connections as the basis of the histories which we acknowledge; to do sociology differently is to act on the basis of having recognized those connections.

II

The reconstruction of categories and understandings argued for here is in direct contrast to the standard methodology of ideal types that is the basis for comparative historical sociology, an approach which is enjoying a revival and whose influence is extensive. New conceptualizations are placed alongside existing ones in a multiplication – rather than reconstruction – of ideal type formulations and are presented as if they have no implications for previous formulations. While ideal types are always presented as, in principle, reformable in light of any new evidence – after all, Weber presents them as 'heuristic' – what appears to occur with much greater frequency, as Holmwood and Stewart (1991) argue, is an attempt to justify the initial selection rather than to account for the new material within revised conceptual categories and explanatory frameworks. This is because ideal types are presented as interpretations that can be regarded as 'valid' despite the 'deviation' of empirical circumstances from the processes represented within the type. Since ideal types are necessarily selective, those other circumstances can be represented within another, different ideal type, which merely sits alongside other ideal types as part of the conceptual armoury of interpretations that are dependent on the purposes at hand. However, the extent to which an ideal type is distinguished from empirical reality, Holmwood and Stewart (1991) continue, further points to the significance of an evaluative and prescriptive element that is also embodied within it. The failure to reconstruct ideal types in light of new evidence suggests not only a commitment to the theoretical construct separate from its relation to the empirical, but also a commitment to the evaluative scheme associated with it.

The ideal type of European modernity, for example, is established on the basis of a selection of historical narratives that simultaneously presents a normative argument about European progress and superiority. This is the 'value-relevant' engagement from which its associated ideal types have been constructed. Any criticism of that selection, in terms of significant histories that may have been omitted in the construction of the type, or that may contradict the evaluative scheme, can be deflected by arguing that what is being proposed is a new set of 'value-relevant' concerns, together with their selective focus, but that the representations that ensue do not call into question those gathered under previous and different value-relevant concerns. To the extent that criticism has ostensibly been addressed, this has led to the development of new ideal types (multiple modernities), that sit alongside the existing type and evaluative scheme, rather than any reconstruction of the original understanding of (European) modernity.[1]

---

[1] Of course, Weber presented his ideal types as heuristic in purpose and, in that context, they could be seen as proto-research programmes (see Papineau 1976). However, this is not how ideal types have been used, not even by Weber in claiming their heuristic purpose. As Brunn (2007) has observed, there are no instances of ideal types reconstructed in the light of their heuristic use.

A methodology of ideal types purports to separate the categories necessary for the construction of valid sociological theories from the value-relevant cultural concerns from which the theoretical gaze issues. In this way, the sociological categories that enter into ideal types are glossed as universal in their nature while being directed at particular (cultural) concerns. Thus, theorists of multiple modernities argue that the concepts to be used in understanding modernity can achieve a form of universalism while allowing different orientations to modernity deriving from different value-relevant interests, including the different value-relevant interests of sociologists located in other cultural settings. This separation establishes an in-principle possibility of agreement on 'facts' and 'consequences', while value-relevant interests need not be resolvable as they derive from factors specific to cultures. In this way, a form of cultural relativism is admitted, while denying its significance for explanatory undertakings. That is, problems that may arise within 'universal' explanations as identified by others, such as Eurocentrism, can be attributed to culturally specific concerns which may be relevant to those subscribing to particular cultural values, but need not concern others subscribing to other cultural values. This establishes a double form of protection for European explanations given the conflation of European cultural values with issues of universal relevance. These explanations cannot be challenged as they constitute the 'facts' and any challenge does not have to be admitted because it is held to derive from the value structures of other cultures.

Interestingly, as I have argued, and revealing the dominance of ideal type methodology within a variety of sociological approaches, this is not only an issue within European historical sociology, but also informs much work on global sociology done from various locations around the world. The key issue for many global sociologists, unsurprisingly, appears to be an assertion of the histories and cultures neglected within the ideal type of (European) modernity. This is often done, however, without challenging the underlying historical narrative that maintains civilizations as distinct entities prior to European encounter and subordinates those civilizations to that encounter. While there may be some critique of the airbrushed narratives of European 'impact', this is not taken as the basis of reconstructing understandings of modernity. Rather, new ideal types of the modernity of other civilizations are developed and placed alongside the existing one. This proliferation of ideal types enables the telling of other histories, but does little to challenge the hierarchies of the established order embodied in the grand ideal type of European modernity. It enables scholars working on and in parts of the world other than Europe and the West access to the privileges of a Eurocentred international academy where space is found for other thinkers and episodes of history that make no difference to the stories Europe otherwise tells of its past.

A critique of Eurocentrism requires also, as Walter Mignolo (2014) argues, a critique of the processes of knowledge production centred upon a European academy writ large. That is, it requires a commitment to the production of knowledge that is decolonial in intent and practice. This means deconstructing the standard narratives based upon the universalization of parochial European histories and reconstructing global narratives on the basis of the empirical connections forged through histories of colonialism, enslavement, dispossession and appropriation.

Global sociology, however, for the most part, appears to display a sensibility that suggests that we have moved past the time when an accounting of such processes was necessary, or that there is no longer a wish to dwell on the past and a preference instead to focus on the construction of new futures. The turn away from grand narratives and towards forms of cultural sociology (or sociologies of culture) enables an ecumenical form of sociology that admits of diffuse and diverse particularities without having to account for how those particularities continue to be framed by the narratives that are now ignored but remain uncontested (see, for example, Adams *et al.* 2005). There is no consideration of how a proper address of these newly identified particularities may provoke a reconsideration of what we had previously thought. In this way, global sociology adds 'new' data to the corpus of our existing knowledge and understanding but does not address the fact that this new data is not really new, just newly added to sociology. My argument here, building on the work of scholars such as Trouillot (1995) and Keita (2002), is that given this new data was not previously unknown or lost, but rather it was associated with peoples and experiences not regarded as significant within dominant accounts, then it cannot simply be brought into sociology without also re-examining the adequacy of those existing narratives. This re-examination should also lead to a reconstruction, on the basis of the new data, of narratives in common. It is this process of reshaping shared narratives in light of what is presented as new data and accounting for why it is understood as new that opens up the space for further insights about historical and social processes.

III

In this book, I have sought to show that the different 'facts' and 'consequences' of interest to sociologists in different social and cultural contexts are mutually implicated and the selections made from the perspective of different cultural contexts cannot be so easily insulated from their explanatory consequences. In this section, I want to consider the same issue from the perspective of the supposed relativism attributed to value-relevant selections of explanatory objects. On the one hand, it appears straightforward that approaches such as multiple modernities (and by implication, those other approaches within global sociology that utilize its formulations), by allowing different cultural inflections of modernity, must necessarily allow different sociologies reflecting those cultural differences (so long, of course, that 'facts' and 'consequences' are accepted). However, as I have already pointed out, the idea of an originary – factual – modernity associated with Europe is also associated with cultural values that claim universality.

This is most obviously the case in arguments about the significance of human rights within the European tradition and also of cosmopolitanism as a defining feature of that tradition. Other cultures may, of course, be represented as offering different 'choices', which, in line with the separation of fact and value that is otherwise being promoted, cannot be 'rationally' resolved. Nonetheless, since these other 'choices' usually entail various forms of authoritarianism, the moral high ground is clear. Further, in this process, authoritarianism is separated from the European tradition, being, at worst, a pathological form reflecting an atavism that lies outside the practices and processes associated with the realization of cosmopolitan human rights. It is precisely here that connected sociologies and their alternative connected histories enable us to pose a challenge to this self-regarding view of the 'European' tradition.

The cosmopolitan commitment of European modernity is presented historically, as emerging from the European tradition of the Enlightenment (although having roots all the way back to ancient Greece), as well as contemporaneously, through the project of European unification in the post-war period. The separation between ideas and practice enables acknowledgement of the interregnum in cosmopolitan practice enforced by the two world wars, and, in particular, the Holocaust, as well as maintaining continuity to some idea of European civilization. The multiple modernities paradigm further presents fascism and Communism as two pathological varieties of modernity, as deviant forms, that may have emerged from a common culture, but whose political expression has no decisive consequence for that culture or for understandings of that culture. That is, these authoritarian forms are not seen to impinge upon the integrity of European modernity as understood in its originary form, or to have any implications for its subsequent development as the hoped for 'finished project' of European modernity (Bauman's (1989) critique in relation to the Holocaust notwithstanding).

The turn to political cosmopolitanism in the post-war period, for example, is presented, for the most part, as a 'return' by Europeans and not as an address of the problems identified through recognition of fascism as a constitutive part of European culture. By identifying fascism as a (uniquely) deviant form, it can simply be bracketed off from the more general histories of Europe that are seen to establish its civilizational qualities. A more adequate reckoning of European fascism, for example, would connect its particular manifestation in Europe with earlier and long-standing forms outwith Europe, namely with the colonial relationships of European states with other parts of the world.

While there may be some belated acknowledgement of authoritarian practice in Europe, by not connecting this to the long-standing and wider practices of authoritarianism enacted by Europe upon much of the rest of the world, the lie of European modernity as based upon a commitment to cosmopolitan values remains firmly in place. It allows partial acknowledgement within European history of a deviant and exceptional period which, in its very uniqueness, means that the condition of European authoritarianism cannot be generalized and made sense of in its generality. European modernity, it seems, is only to be defined in terms of its cultural ideas about itself and in terms of the histories it chooses to acknowledge as significant and not in terms of those it does not.

So, historically, the French and industrial revolutions make the cut, but not the processes of colonialism, enslavement, dispossession and appropriation that constitute the conditions of their very possibility. And, contemporaneously, the peaceable character of European cosmopolitan civilization is established on the basis of refraining from killing other white Europeans, but does not take into account the millions of people killed in the execution of the European project who were not white – the Algerians, the Mau Mau, the Congolese, among countless others (for discussion, see Hansen 2002, 2004; Bhambra 2009). What enables this severe form of disjunctive recognition, whereby a cosmopolitan commitment is lauded despite the countless historical and contemporary arguments against its very plausibility, is, in part, the Weberian model of historical sociology. This model, based on ideal types as discussed above, actively discourages address of problems identified by others concerning the legitimacy and adequacy of the 'facts' and 'consequences' of European modernity. In the following section, I discuss how taking such challenges seriously could enable the development of a sociology more adequate to the address of contemporary problems.

IV

The idea of the political community as a *national* political order has been central to European self-understanding and to European historical sociology. Yet many European states were imperial states as much as they were national states – and often prior to or alongside becoming national states – and so the political community of the state was always much broader and more stratified than is usually acknowledged. The history of the British nation state, for example, usually starts with the Act of Union in 1707, which brought together the kingdoms of England and Scotland, and its political development is predominantly seen in terms of events and processes that took place within the territorial bounds of the new nation. However, both England and Scotland had acquired colonies prior to Union, and continued their colonial conquests after Union, and so they were already imperial states prior to becoming a nation state – and alongside this process (Colley 1992, 2002). Empire, however, is not deemed to be significant for understanding the history or contemporary society of the nation state, as we have seen in the discussion of the work of historical-sociologists such as Wallerstein or Mann in an earlier chapter. One consequence of this is that, while the political community of the British Empire was a multicultural community historically, this understanding rarely enters contemporary political discourse where the boundaries of political community are imagined as congruent with the territorial boundaries of the state as understood in national terms.

The failure to acknowledge these multicultural histories of colonialism and empire as pertinent to our understandings of the contemporary political state can be seen to have political repercussions in the debates on immigration that disfigure most national elections in Europe. Elections mark a period of time when the terms of the political contracts that bind people together are up for negotiation. What is important to note is, that while these contracts are about the negotiation of *present* conditions, these negotiations occur in the context of particular *historical* narratives of belonging. These narratives are usually structured in terms of presumed originary members of the contract or political community and *their* rights in contrast to those of 'newcomers' or migrants. Migrants are, by definition, excluded from the history of the state understood in national terms and thus from the history of belonging to the political community. By being excluded from the *history* of political community, these 'newcomers' or migrants are also excluded from rights within the polity and excluded from the right to renegotiate the terms of that polity. That is, while they may have rights to be *included* (though these are often also denied), they are not presumed to have rights *to redraw the terms or limits* of the political community as currently instituted.

While the political contract is usually understood in terms of national state boundaries, as I have argued, European states did not bind themselves in this way, but were active in colonial projects with more extensive boundaries. If, then, we understand the histories of the nation state as broader than the accounts of activities of its supposedly 'indigenous' inhabitants, then the arbitrary reduction of history to contemporary national boundaries can be seen to misidentify those associated with more expansive histories as migrants, instead of seeing them more properly as citizens. That is, those identified as 'migrant' or 'other' within national states were not necessarily 'other' at the point of arrival. They often came as citizens, or at the very least as subjects, of these broader political configurations, namely empires.

The occlusions at national level across Europe are curiously inverted at the common European level where all unbounded histories are assigned to the histories of individual states, and not to the history of 'Europe'. For example, a Europe 'free of war' as a consequence of the post-war European project is not a Europe whose member states were not at war – for example, a civil war in France, involving 'departments' (Algeria) claiming (rightful) independence, is not mentioned nor does it negate the identification of Europe as peaceable (Hansen 2002). Colonialism becomes the past property of individual nation states to be displaced by a new narrative of European integration free from the stain of colonialism (for a discussion of the centrality of colonialism to the European project, however, see Hansen and Jonsson (2014)). By erasing the colonial past, the postcolonial present of Europe and European states is also disavowed.

Following Said (1995), then, I am arguing for recognition of inter-twined histories and overlapping territories as a more adequate basis for the development of our conceptual categories than purified national histories. One consequence of this would be to understand migration to Europe as integral to the narrative of national, and European, identity; that is, to understand migration as central and as constitutive of the histories of the state as otherwise told – and to understand migrants also as citizens historically, not just as potential citizens-in-waiting. As I have already noted, in the British context, a significant part of the cement that bound its component countries together was that a professional and middle class from peripheral areas could find occupation in the colonies – a migratory history that is acknowledged in national accounts, while that of those they governed or administered is not. Standard presenta-tions of European cosmopolitanism rarely take account of the diversity *within* Europe as constituted by (migrant) minorities within states. My argument is that taking account of this diversity enables us to tell different histories of Europe which then open up the possibility of different political solutions to the urgent questions of the time.

V

In sum, global sociology, I argue, is best served by a sociology of connections that takes seriously the histories of interconnection that have enabled the world to emerge as a global space. Global sociology acknowledges the masquerade of European histories as world-historical upon which sociology has largely been constructed and seeks to reconstruct sociology on the basis of more adequate historical understandings. It is more than a history of (long-standing) globalization, however. It points to a sociology that starts from the perspective of the world by locating itself within the processes that facilitated the emergence of that world. By starting from a location in the world, necessarily means starting from a history that enabled that location to be part of the world; identifying and explicating the connections that enable understandings always to be more expansive than the identities or events they are seeking to explain. As Holmwood and Stewart argue in a different context, but applicable here all the same, 'the important point is not to *reify* the new explanation, but to indicate how it was produced by turning towards explanatory problems, rather than away from them, and creating new understandings and resources in their solution' (1991: 61). If the key problem identified through this book has been the particular, parochial configurations of the global within sociology, any new understanding of the global cannot simply be asserted, but has to be argued for in terms of how it addresses the deficiencies and limitations of previous understandings and how it enables more productive insights in the future.

This book is a critique of sociology, but it also expresses a commitment to an expanded sociological imagination. As I mentioned in the Introduction, critique often engenders resistance and a perception by those who see themselves as subject to criticism that they are faced with a potential loss of meaning. But what is being criticized are structures of meaning and their limitations. The promise of constructive criticism is expanded meaning. These aspects are well captured in Fanon's conclusion to *The Wretched of the Earth*, where he exhorts: 'Come, then, comrades, the European game has finally ended; we must find something different' (1968 [1961]: 252). A particular way of doing things is potentially over, but its recognition is inclusive and comradely. It is not a puncturing of meaning, but of hierarchy, and a call to reconstruct meaning and to engage in new collective endeavours.

Bibliography

Abbott, Andrew 1991. 'History and Sociology: The Lost Synthesis', *Social Science History* 15 (2): 201–38.

Abrams, Philip 1980. 'History, Sociology, Historical Sociology', *Past and Present* 87 (May): 3–16.

Adams, Julia, Elisabeth S. Clemens and Ann Shola Orloff (eds) 2005. *Remaking Modernity: Politics, History and Sociology*. Durham, NC: Duke University Press.

Adesina, Jimi O. 2002. 'Sociology and Yoruba Studies: Epistemic Intervention or Doing Sociology in the "Vernacular"?', *African Sociological Review* 6 (1): 91–114.

Akiwowo, Akinsola A. 1986. 'Contributions to the Sociology of Knowledge from an African Oral Poetry', *International Sociology* 1 (4): 343–58.

—1988. 'Universalism and Indigenisation in Sociological Theory: Introduction', *International Sociology* 3 (2): 155–60.

—1999. 'Indigenous Sociologies: Extending the Scope of the Argument', *International Sociology* 14 (20): 115–38.

Alatas, Syed Farid 1993. 'On the Indigenization of Academic Discourse', *Alternatives: Global, Local, Political* 18 (3): 307–38.

—2001. 'Alternative Discourses in Southeast Asia', *Sari* 19: 49–67.

—2006. 'Editorial Introduction: The Idea of Autonomous Sociology: Reflections on the State of the Discipline', *Current Sociology* 54 (1): 5–6.

—2010. 'Religion and Reform: Two Exemplars for Autonomous Sociology in the Non-Western Context', in Sujata Patel (ed.), *The ISA Handbook of Diverse Sociological Traditions*. London: Sage, pp. 29–39.

Alatas, Syed Hussein 1974. 'The Captive Mind and Creative Development', *International Social Science Journal* 36 (4): 691–9.

—1979. 'Towards an Asian Social Science Tradition', *New Quest* 17: 265–9.

—2000. 'Intellectual Imperialism: Definition, Traits, and Problems', *Southeast Asian Journal of Social Science* 28 (1): 23–45.

—2002. 'The Development of an Autonomous Social Science Tradition in Asia: Problems and Prospects', *Asian Journal of Social Science* 30 (1): 150–7.

—2006. 'The Autonomous, the Universal and the Future of Sociology', *Current Sociology* 54 (1): 7–23.

Alavi, Hamza 1964. 'Imperialism Old and New', *Socialist Register* 1: 14–126.

Albrow, Martin 1990. 'Introduction', in Martin Albrow and Elizabeth King (eds), *Globalization, Knowledge and Society*. London: Sage, pp. 3–13.

Albrow, Martin and Elizabeth King (eds) 1990. *Globalization, Knowledge and Society*. London: Sage.

Alexander, Jeffrey C. 1995. *Fin de Siècle Social Theory: Relativism, Reduction and the Problem of Reason*. London: Verso.

Almond, Gabriel A. and James S. Coleman (eds) 1960. *The Politics of Developing Areas*. Princeton, NJ: Princeton University Press.

Amin, Ash 2004. 'Multi-Ethnicity and the Idea of Europe', *Theory, Culture and Society* 21 (2): 1–24.

Amin, Samir 1973 [1971]. *Neocolonialism in West Africa*, translated by Francis McDonagh. London: Penguin Books.

Anderson, Perry 1974. *Lineages of the Absolutist State*. London: Verso.

Appiah, A. 1992. *In My Father's House: Africa in the Philosophy of Culture*. Oxford: Oxford University Press.

Archer, Margaret S. 1991. 'Presidential Address: Sociology for One World: Unity and Diversity', *International Sociology* 6 (2): 131–47.

Arjomand, Said Amir 2000. '*International Sociology* into the New Millennium: The Global Sociological Community and the Challenge to the Periphery', *International Sociology* 15 (1): 5–10.

—2011. Review: Sujata Patel (ed.), *The ISA Handbook of Diverse Sociological Traditions*, Sage: London, 2010; 366, *International Sociology Review of Books* 26 (2): 197–200.

Arnason, Johann P. 2000. 'Communism and Modernity', *Daedalus* 129 (1): 61–90.

—2003. 'Entangled Communisms: Imperial Revolutions in Russia and China', *European Journal of Social Theory* 6 (3): 307–25.

Asad, Talal 1979. 'Anthropology and the Colonial Encounter', in Gerrit Huizer and Bruce Mannheim (eds), *The Politics of Anthropology: From Colonialism and Sexism Toward a View from Below*. The Hague: Mouten Publishers, pp. 85–94.

Babu, A. M. 1972. 'Postscript', in Walter Rodney *How Europe Underdeveloped Africa*. London: Bogle-L'Ouverture Publication and Dar-es-Salaam: Tanzania Publishing House.

Bakewell, Peter John 1971. *Silver Mining and Society in Colonial Mexico: Zacatecas, 1546–1700*. Cambridge: Cambridge University Press.

Bauman, Zygmunt 1989. *Modernity and the Holocaust*. Cambridge: Polity Press.

Beck, U. 2000. 'The Cosmopolitan Perspective: Sociology of the Second Age of Modernity', *British Journal of Sociology* 51 (1): 79–105.

—2002. 'The Cosmopolitan Society and Its Enemies', *Theory Culture Society* 19 (1–2): 17–44.

—2006. *Cosmopolitan Vision*. Cambridge: Polity Press.

Beck, U. and E. Grande 2007. 'Cosmopolitanism: Europe's Way Out of Crisis', *European Journal of Social Theory* 10 (1): 67–85.

Behbehanian, Laleh and Michael Burawoy 2011. 'Global Sociology: Reflections on an Experimental Course', *Global Sociology, Live!* http://globalsociologylive.blogspot.co.uk/ (accessed 1 March 2014).

Bernstein, Henry 1971. 'Modernization Theory and the Sociological Study of Development', *Journal of Development Studies* 7 (2): 141–60.

—1976 [1973]. 'Introduction', in *Underdevelopment and Development: The Third World Today. Selected Readings*. London: Penguin Books, pp. 13–30.

Bhabha, Homi K. 1994. *The Location of Culture*. London: Routledge.

Bhambra, Gurminder K. 2007. *Rethinking Modernity: Postcolonialism and the Sociological Imagination*. Basingstoke: Palgrave Macmillan.

—2010. 'Historical Sociology, International Relations and Connected Histories', *Cambridge Review of International Affairs* 23 (1): 127–43.

—2011a. 'Talking among Themselves? Weberian and Marxist Historical Sociologies as Dialogues without "Others"', *Millennium: Journal of International Studies* 39 (3): 667–81.

—2011b. 'Historical Sociology, Modernity, and Postcolonial Critique', *American Historical Review* 116 (3): 653–62.

—2011c. 'Cosmopolitanism and Postcolonial Critique', in M. Rovisco and M. Nowicka (eds), *The Ashgate Companion to Cosmopolitanism*. Farnham: Ashgate, pp. 313–28.

—2014. 'A Sociological Dilemma: Race, Segregation, and US Sociology', *Current Sociology* 62 (4): tba.

Booth, David 1985. 'Marxism and Development Sociology: Interpreting the Impasse', *World Development* 13 (7): 761–87.

Braudel, Fernand 1981. *Civilization and Capitalism, 15th–18th Century*, Volume 1: *The Structures of Everyday Life*, translated by Siân Reynolds. London: William Collins & Sons.

—1982. *Civilization and Capitalism, 15th–18th Century*, Volume 2: *The Wheels of Commerce*, translated by Siân Reynolds. London: William Collins & Sons.

—1985. *Civilization and Capitalism, 15th–18th Century*, Volume 3: *The Perspective of the World*, translated by Siân Reynolds. London: Fontana Press.

Brenner, Robert 1976. 'Agrarian Class Structure and Economic Development in Pre-Industrial Europe', *Past and Present* 70 (February): 30–75.

—1977. 'The Origins of Capitalist Development: A Critique of Neo-Smithian Marxism', *New Left Review* 104: 25–92.

Briceño-León, Roberto and Heinz R. Sonntag 1997a. 'Introduction: Latin American Sociology Caught between People, Time and Development', in Roberto Briceño-León and Heinz R. Sonntag (eds), *Sociology in Latin America*. Proceedings of the ISA Regional Conference for Latin America. http://www.isa-sociology.org/colmemb/national-associations/en/meetings/reports/Latin%20American%20Sociology.pdf (accessed 1 March 2014).

—1997b. *Sociology in Latin America*. Proceedings of the ISA Regional Conference for Latin America. http://www.isa-sociology.org/colmemb/national-associations/en/meetings/reports/Latin%20American%20Sociology.pdf (accessed 1 March 2014).

Brown, Kendall W. 2012. *A History of Mining in Latin America: From the Colonial Era to the Present*. Albuquerque, NM: University of New Mexico Press.

Brunn, Hans H. 2007. *Science, Values, and Politics in Max Weber's Methodology*. Aldershot: Ashgate.

Burawoy, Michael 2005a. 'For Public Sociology', *American Sociological Review* 70 (February): 4–28.

—2005b. 'Conclusion: Provincializing the Social Sciences', in George Steinmetz (ed.), *The Politics of Method in the Human Sciences*. Durham, NC, and London: Duke University Press, pp. 508–25.

—2008. 'Rejoinder: For a Subaltern Global Sociology', *Current Sociology* 56 (3): 435–44.

—2010a. 'Facing an Unequal World: Challenges for a Global Sociology', in Michael Burawoy, Mau-kuei Chang and Michelle Fei-yu Hsieh (eds), *Facing an Unequal World: Challenge for a Global Sociology*. Taipei: Academica Sinica and International Sociological Association, pp. 3–27.

—2010b. 'Forging Global Sociology from Below', in Sujata Patel (ed.), *The ISA Handbook of Diverse Sociological Traditions*. London: Sage, pp. 52–65.

Burawoy, Michael, Mau-kuei Chang and Michelle Fei-yu Hsieh (eds) 2010. *Facing an Unequal World: Challenge for a Global Sociology* (3 vols). Taipei: Academica Sinica and International Sociological Association.

Cardoso, Fernando H. 1972. 'Dependency and Development in Latin America', *New Left Review* 74 (July–August): 83–95.

Césaire, Aimé 1972 [1955]. *Discourse on Colonialism*, translated by Joan Pinkham. New York: Monthly Review Press.

Chakrabarty, Dipesh 2000. *Provincializing Europe: Postcolonial Thought and Historical Difference*. Princeton, NJ: Princeton University Press.

Chernilo, Daniel 2007. *A Social Theory of the Nation State: Beyond Methodological Nationalism*. London: Routledge.

Christian, David 2003. 'World History in Context', *Journal of World History* 14 (4): 437–52.

Cole, Jeffrey A. 1985. *The Potosí Mita: Compulsory Indian Labor in the Andes*. Stanford, CA: Stanford University Press.

Colley, Linda 1992. *Britons: Forging the Nation 1707–1837*. New Haven, CT: Yale University Press.

—2002. *Captives: Britain, Empire and the World 1600–1850*. New York: Pantheon Books.

Connell, Raewyn 1997. 'Why is Classical Theory Classical?', *American Journal of Sociology* 102 (6): 1511–57.

—2007a. *Southern Theory: The Global Dynamics of Knowledge in Social Science*. Cambridge: Polity Press.

—2007b. 'The Northern Theory of Globalization', *Sociological Theory* 25 (4): 368–85.

—2010. 'Learning from Each Other: Sociology on a World Scale', in Sujata Patel (ed.), *The ISA Handbook of Diverse Sociological Traditions*. London: Sage, pp. 52–65.

Cox, Oliver C. 1970 [1948]. *Caste, Class and Race: A Study in Social Dynamics*. New York: Modern Reader Paperback.

Dean, Britten 1976. 'British Informal Empire: The Case of China', *The Journal of Commonwealth & Comparative Politics* 14 (1): 64–81.

Demir, Ipek 2011. 'Lost in Translation? Try Second Language Learning: Understanding Movements of Ideas and Practices across Time and Space', *Journal of Historical Sociology* 24 (1): 9–26.

Depelchin, Jacques 2005. *Silences in African History: Between the Syndromes of Discovery and Abolition*. Dar-es-Salaam: Mkuki na Nyota Publishers.

Dirlik, Arif 2003. 'Global Modernity? Modernity in an Age of Global Capitalism', *European Journal of Social Theory* 6(3): 275–92.

Dos Santos, Theotonio 1970. 'The Structure of Dependence', *The American Economic Review* 60 (2): 231–36.

Driver, Felix 1992. 'Geography's Empire: Histories of Geographical Knowledge', *Environment and Planning D: Society and Space* 10 (1): 23–40.

DuBois, W. E. B. 1935. *Black Reconstruction: An Essay toward a History of the Part which Black Folk Played in the Attempt to Reconstruct Democracy in America, 1860–1880*. Philadelphia, PA: Albert Saifer Publisher.

Dudziak, Mary L. 1988. 'Desegregation as a Cold War Imperative', *Stanford Law Review* 41 (1): 61–120.

Dussel, Enrique 2008. 'Philosophy of Liberation, the Postmodern Debate, and Latin American Studies', in Mabel Morana, Enrique Dussel and Carlos A. Jauregui (eds), *Coloniality at Large: Latin America and the Postcolonial Debate*. Durham, NC: Duke University Press, pp. 335–49.

Eisenstadt, Shmuel N. 1965. 'Transformation of Social, Political, and Cultural Orders in Modernization', *American Sociological Review* 30 (5): 659–73.

—1974. 'Studies of Modernization and Sociological Theory', *History and Theory* 13 (3): 225–52.

—1992. 'The Breakdown of Communist Regimes and the Vicissitudes of Modernity', *Daedalus* 121 (2): 21–41.

—2000a. 'Multiple Modernities', *Daedalus* 129 (1): 1–29.

—2000b. 'The Civilizational Dimension in Sociological Analysis', *Thesis Eleven* 62: 1–21.

Eisenstadt, S. N. and W. Schluchter 1998. 'Introduction: Paths to Early Modernities – A Comparative View'. *Daedalus* 127 (3): 1–18.

Ellison, Ralph 1973 [1944]. 'An American Dilemma: A Review', in Joyce A. Ladner (ed.), *The Death of White Sociology*. New York: Vintage Books, pp. 81–95.

Emmanuel, Arghiri 1974. 'Myths of Development versus Myths of Underdevelopment', *New Left Review* 1 (85): 61–82.

Falola, Toyin 2005. 'Writing and Teaching National History in Africa in an Era of Global History', *Africa Spectrum* 40: 499–519.

Fals Borda, Orlando 1980. 'The Negation of Sociology and Its Promise: Perspectives of Social Science in Latin America Today', *Latin American Research Review* 15 (1): 161–6.

Fanon, Frantz 1963. *The Wretched of the Earth*, translated by Constance Farrington. New York: Grove Press.

—1967 [1952]. *Black Skin, White Masks*, translated by Charles Lam Markmann. New York: Grove Press.

Fine, Robert 2007. *Cosmopolitanism*. London: Routledge.

Fourcade, Marion 2009. *Economists and Societies: Discipline and Profession in the United States, Britain, and France, 1890s to 1990s*. Princeton, NJ: Princeton University Press.

Frank, Andre Gunder 1970. *Latin America: Underdevelopment of Revolution. Essays on the Development of Underdevelopment and the Immediate Enemy*. New York: Monthly Review.

Frazier, E. Franklin 1947. 'Sociological Theory and Race Relations', *American Sociological Review* 12 (3): 265–71.

Fukuyama, Francis 1992. *The End of History and the Last Man*. New York: The Free Press.

Galeano, Eduardo 1973. *Open Veins of Latin America: Five Centuries of the Pillage of a Continent*, translated by Cedric Belfrage. New York: Monthly Review Press.

Gallagher, John and Ronald Robinson 1953. 'The Imperialism of Free Trade', *The Economic History Review* 6 (1): 1–15.

Gandhi, Leela 1998. *Postcolonial Theory: A Critical Introduction*. New York: Columbia University Press.

Gareau, Frederick H. 1988. 'Another Type of Third World Dependency: The Social Sciences', *International Sociology* 3 (2): 171–78.

Gilroy, Paul 1993. *The Black Atlantic: Modernity and Double Consciousness*. Cambridge, MA: Harvard University Press.

Goldthorpe, John 1991. 'The Uses of History in Sociology: Reflections on Some Recent Tendencies', *British Journal of Sociology* 42 (2): 211–30.

Göle, Nilüfer 2000. 'Snapshots of Islamic Modernities', *Daedalus* 129 (1): 91–117.

Goody, Jack 2006. *The Theft of History*. Cambridge: Cambridge University Press.

Greenberg, Michael 1951. *British Trade and the Opening of China 1800–1842*. Cambridge: Cambridge University Press.

Grosfoguel, Ramon 2000. 'Developmentalism, Modernity, and Dependency Theory in Latin America', *Nepantla: Views from the South* 1 (2): 347–73.

Guha, Ranajit 1982. 'On Some Aspects of the Historiography of Colonial India', in Ranajit Guha (ed.), *Subaltern Studies: Writings on South Asian History and Society*, Volume 1. Delhi: Oxford University Press, pp. 1–8.

—1983. 'The Prose of Counter-Insurgency', in Ranajit Guha (ed.), *Subaltern Studies: Writings on South Asian History and Society*, Volume 2. Delhi: Oxford University Press, pp. 1–42.

Habermas, Jurgen 1984. *The Theory of Communicative Action*, Volume I: *Reason and the Rationalization of Society*. London: Heinemann.

—1988. *On the Logic of the Social Sciences*. Cambridge: Polity Press.

Hall, Stuart 1992. 'The West and the Rest: Discourse and Power', in Stuart Hall and Brian Gieben (eds), *Formations of Modernity*. Cambridge: Polity Press/Open University.

Hansen, Peo 2002. 'European Integration, European Identity and the Colonial Connection', *European Journal of Social Theory* 5 (4): 483–98.

—2004. 'In the Name of Europe', *Race and Class* 45 (3): 49–62.

Hansen, Peo and Stefan Jonsson 2014. *Eurafrica: The Untold History of European Integration and Colonialism*. London: Bloomsbury Academic.

Hobson, John A. 1954 [1902]. *Imperialism: A Study*. London: George Allen & Unwin.

Hobson, John M. 2004. *The Eastern Origins of Western Civilisation*. Cambridge: Cambridge University Press.

Holmwood, John 1998. 'Review: A Treatise on Social Theory, Volume III: Applied Social Theory', *The British Journal of Sociology* 49 (3): 507–8.

—2000a. 'Sociology and Its Audience(s): Changing Perceptions of Sociological Argument', in John Eldridge *et al.* (eds), *For Sociology: Legacies and Prospects*. Durham, UK: Sociology Press.

—2000b. 'Europe and the "Americanization" of British Social Policy', *European Societies* 2 (4), 453–82.

—2013. 'Public Reasoning without Sociology: Amartya Sen's Theory of Justice', *Sociology* 47 (6): 1171–86.

Holmwood, John and Alexander Stewart 1991. *Explanation and Social Theory*. London: Macmillan.

Irwin, Robert 2007. *For Lust of Knowing: The Orientalists and their Enemies*. London: Penguin Books.

Jennings, Francis 1971. 'Virgin Land and Savage People', *American Quarterly* 23 (4): 519–41.

Joshi, P. C. 1986. 'Founders of the Lucknow School and Their Legacy: Radhakamal Mukerjee and D. P. Mukerji: Some Reflections', *Economic and Political Weekly* 21 (33): 1455–1469.

Kaya, Ibrahim 2004. 'Modernity, Openness, Interpretation: A Perspective on Multiple Modernities', *Social Science Information* 43 (1): 35–57.

Keim, Wiebke 2008. 'Social Sciences Internationally: The Problem of Marginalisation and Its Consequences for the Discipline of Sociology', *African Sociological Review* 12 (2): 22–48.

—2011. 'Counterhegemonic Currents and Internationalisation of Sociology: Theoretical Reflections and an Empirical Example', *International Sociology* 26 (1): 123–45.

Keita, Maghan 2002. 'Africa and the Construction of a Grand Narrative in World History', in Eckhardt Fuchs and Benedikt Stuchtey (eds), *Across Cultural Borders: Historiography in Global Perspective*. New York: Rowman & Littlefield.

Kelley, Robin D. G. 1999. '"But a Local Phase of a World Problem": Black History's Global Vision, 1883–1950', *The Journal of American History* 86 (3): 1045–77.

King, Desmond and Rogers M. Smith 2011. *Still a House Divided: Race and Politics in Obama's America*. Princeton, NJ: Princeton University Press.

Ladner, Joyce A. (ed.) 1973. *The Death of White Sociology*. New York: Vintage Books.

Lall, Sanjaya 1975. 'Is "Dependence" a Useful Concept in Analysing Underdevelopment?', *World Development* 3 (11–12): 799–810.

Lamont, Michèle and Sada Aksartova 2002. 'Ordinary Cosmopolitanisms: Strategies for Bridging Racial Boundaries among Working-Class Men', *Theory, Culture and Society* 19 (4): 1–25.

Lander, Edgardo 1997. 'Eurocentrism and Colonialism in the Latin American Social Thought', in Roberto Briceño-León and Heinz R. Sonntag (eds), *Sociology in Latin America*. Proceedings of the ISA Regional Conference for Latin America. http://www.isa-sociology.org/colmemb/national-associations/en/meetings/reports/Latin%20American%20Sociology.pdf (accessed 1 March 2014).

Lawuyi, O. B. and Olufemi Taiwo 1990. 'Towards an African Sociological Tradition: A Rejoinder to Akiwowo and Makinde', in M. Albrow and

E. King (eds), *Globalization, Knowledge and Society*. London: Sage, pp. 101–54.

Lerner, Daniel 1958. *The Passing of Traditional Society: Modernizing the Middle East*. New York: The Free Press.

Levy, Marion J. 1965. 'Patterns (Structures) of Modernization and Political Development', *Annals of the American Academy of Political and Social Science* 358 (1): 29–40.

Leys, Colin 1977. 'Underdevelopment and Dependency: Critical Notes', *Journal of Contemporary Asia* 7 (1): 92–107.

Loomba, Ania 2005 [1998]. *Colonialism/Postcolonialism*. Second edition. London and New York: Routledge.

Lorde, Audre 2007. *Sister Outsider: Essays and Speeches*. Berkeley, CA: The Crossing Press.

Lugones, María 2007. 'Heterosexualism and the Colonial/Modern Gender System', *Hypatia* 22 (1): 186–209.

—2011. 'Toward a Decolonial Feminism', *Hypatia* 25 (4): 742–59.

McNeill, William H. 1990. 'The Rise of the West after Twenty-Five Years', *Journal of World History* 1 (1): 1–21.

MacKenzie, John M. 1995. *Orientalism: History, Theory and the Arts*. Manchester: Manchester University Press.

Makinde, M. Akin 1990. 'Asuwada Principle: An Analysis of Akiwowo's Contributions to the Sociology of Knowledge from an African Perspective', in Martin Albrow and Elizabeth King (eds), *Globalization, Knowledge and Society*. London: Sage, pp. 119–134.

Maldonado-Torres, Nelson 2007. 'On the Coloniality of Being: Contributions to the Development of a Concept', *Cultural Studies* 21 (2–3): 240–70.

Mann, Michael 1986. *The Sources of Social Power*, Volume 1: *A History of Power from the Beginning to AD 1760*. Cambridge: Cambridge University Press.

—1993. *The Sources of Social Power*, Volume 2: *The Rise of Classes and Nation states, 1760–1914*. Cambridge: Cambridge University Press.

—2012. *The Sources of Social Power*, Volume 3: *Global Empires and Revolution, 1890–1945*. Cambridge: Cambridge University Press.

—2013. *The Sources of Social Power*, Volume 4: *Globalisations, 1945–2011*. Cambridge: Cambridge University Press.

Marx, Karl 1976 [1867]. *Capital: A Critique of Political Economy*, Volume 1, introduced by Ernest Mandel, translated by Ben Fowkes. London: Penguin Books.

Mayblin, Lucy 2013. 'Never Look Back: Political Thought and the Abolition of Slavery', *Cambridge Review of International Affairs* 26 (1): 93–110.

Mazrui, Ali A. 1968. 'From Social Darwinism to Current Theories of Modernization', *World Politics* 21 (1): 69–83.

Memmi, Albert 1965 [1957]. *The Colonizer and the Colonized*. Boston, MA: Beacon Press.

Mignolo, Walter D. 2000. 'The Geopolitics of Knowledge and the Colonial Difference', *South Atlantic Quarterly* 101 (1): 57–96.

—2007a. 'Introduction: Coloniality of Power and De-colonial Thinking', *Cultural Studies* 21 (2): 155–67.

—2007b. 'Delinking: The Rhetoric of Modernity, the Logic of Coloniality and the Grammar of De-coloniality', *Cultural Studies* 21 (2): 449–514.

—2011. *The Darker Side of Western Modernity: Global Futures, Decolonial Options*. Durham, NC: Duke University Press.

—2014. 'Spirit Out of Bounds Returns to the East: The Closing of the Social Sciences and the Opening of Independent Thoughts', *Current Sociology* 62 (4): tba.

Modi, Ishwar 2010. 'Indian Sociology Faces the World', in Michael Burawoy, Mau-kuei Chang and Michelle Fei-yu Hsieh (eds), *Facing an Unequal World: Challenge for a Global Sociology*. Taipei: Academica Sinica and International Sociological Association, pp. 316–25.

Mohanty, Satya P. (ed.) 2011. *Colonialism, Modernity, and Literature: A View from India*. New York: Palgrave Macmillan.

Mongia, Padmini (ed.) 2000. *Contemporary Postcolonial Theory: A Reader*. New Delhi: Oxford University Press India.

Myrdal, Gunnar 1944. *An American Dilemma: The Negro Problem and Modern Democracy*. New York: Harper and Brothers.

O'Brien, Patrick K. and Geoffrey Allen Pigman 1992. 'Free Trade, British Hegemony and the International Economic Order in the Nineteenth Century', *Review of International Studies* 18 (2): 89–113.

Oomen, T. K. 1991. 'Internationalization of Sociology: A View from Developing Countries', *Current Sociology* 39: 85–100.

Palma, Gabriel 1978. 'Dependency: A Formal Theory of Underdevelopment of a Methodology for the Analysis of Concrete Situations of Underdevelopment?', *World Development* 6 (7–8): 881–924.

Papineau, David 1976. 'Ideal Types and Empirical Theories' *British Journal of the Philosophy of Science* 27 (2): 137–46.

Parsons, Talcott 1966. *Societies: Evolutionary and Comparative Perspectives.* Englewood Cliffs, NJ: Prentice Hall.

—1967. 'Introduction: Why "Freedom Now," Not Yesterday?', in Talcott Parsons and Kenneth B. Clark (eds), *The Negro American.* Boston, MA: Beacon Press.

—1971. *The System of Modern Societies.* New Jersey: Prentice Hall.

—2007. *American Society: A Theory of the Societal Community*, edited and introduced by Giuseppe Sciortino. Boulder, CO: Paradigm Publishers.

Parsons, Talcott and Kenneth B. Clark (eds) 1967. *The Negro American.* Boston, MA: Beacon Press.

Patel, Sujata 2006. 'Beyond Binaries: A Case for Self-Reflexive Sociologies', *Current Sociology* 54 (3): 381–95.

—(ed.) 2010a. *The ISA Handbook of Diverse Sociological Traditions.* London: Sage.

—2010b. 'Introduction: Diversities of Sociological Traditions', in Sujata Patel (ed.), *The ISA Handbook of Diverse Sociological Traditions.* London: Sage, pp. 52–65.

—2010c. 'At Crossroads: Sociology in India', in Sujata Patel (ed.), *The ISA Handbook of Diverse Sociological Traditions.* London: Sage, pp. 280–91.

—2010d. 'Sociology's "Other": The Debates on European Universals', in *The Encyclopaedia of Life Support Systems* (Social Sciences and Humanities). UNESCO. www.eolss.net

—2014a 'Gazing Backwards and Looking Forwards: Colonial Modernity and the Making of a Sociology of Modern India', in Said Arjomand (ed.), *Social Theory and Regional Studies.* New York: SUNY Press.

—2014b 'Is There a South Perspective to Urban Studies?', in Susan Parnell and Sophie Oldfield (eds), *Routledge Handbook on Cities of the Global South.* London: Routledge, pp. 37–47.

Pollock, Sheldon, Homi K. Bhabha, Carol Breckenbridge and Dipesh Chakrabarty 2000. 'Cosmopolitanisms', *Public Culture* 12 (3): 577–89.

Pomeranz, Kenneth 2000. *The Great Divergence: China, Europe, and the Making of the Modern World Economy.* Princeton, NJ: Princeton University Press.

Portes, Alejandro 1976. 'On the Sociology of National Development: Theories and Issues', *American Journal of Sociology* 82 (1): 55–85.

Prashad, Vijay 2007. *The Darker Nations: A People's History of the Third World.* New York: The New Press.

Quijano, Aníbal 1971. *Nationalism & Capitalism in Peru: A Study in Neo-Imperialism*, translated by Helen R. Lane. London: Monthly Review Press.

—1997. 'The Colonial Nature of Power and Latin America's Cultural Experience', in Roberto Briceño-León and Heinz R. Sonntag (eds), *Sociology in Latin America*. Proceedings of the ISA Regional Conference for Latin America. http://www.isa-sociology.org/colmemb/national-associations/en/meetings/reports/Latin%20American%20Sociology.pdf (accessed 1 March 2014).

—2007. 'Coloniality and Modernity/Rationality', *Cultural Studies* 21 (2): 168–78.

Ray, Larry 1997. 'Post-Communism: Postmodernity or Modernity Revisited?', *British Journal of Sociology* 48 (4): 543–60.

Robinson, William I. 1998. 'Beyond Nation-State Paradigms: Globalization, Sociology, and the Challenge of Transnational Studies', *Sociological Forum* 13 (4): 561–94.

—2011. 'Globalization and the Sociology of Immanuel Wallerstein: A Critical Appraisal', *International Sociology* 26 (6): 723–45.

Rodney, Walter 1972. *How Europe Underdeveloped Africa*. London: Bogle-L'Ouverture Publication and Dar-es-Salaam: Tanzania Publishing House.

Rostow, Walt W. 1960. *The Stages of Economic Growth: A Non-Communist Manifesto*. Cambridge: Cambridge University Press.

Runciman, W. Garry 1997. *A Treatise on Social Theory*, Volume 3: *Applied Social Theory*. Cambridge: Cambridge University Press.

Said, Edward W. 1994. *Culture and Imperialism*. London: Chatto & Windus.

—1995 [1978]. *Orientalism: Western Conceptions of the Orient*, with a new afterword. London: Penguin Books.

Saint-Arnaud, Pierre 2009. *African American Pioneers of Sociology: A Critical History*, translated by Peter Feldstein. Toronto, ON: University of Toronto Press.

Santos, Boaventura de Sousa 2001. 'Nuestra America: Reinventing a Subaltern Paradigm of Recognition and Redistribution', *Theory, Culture & Society* 18 (2–3): 185–217.

—2006. 'Globalizations', *Theory, Culture & Society* 23 (2–3): 393–9.

—(ed.) 2007a. *Another Knowledge is Possible: Beyond Northern Epistemologies*. London: Verso.

—2007b. 'Human Rights as an Emancipatory Script? Cultural and Political Conditions', in Boaventura de Sousa Santos (ed.), *Another Knowledge is Possible: Beyond Northern Epistemologies*. London: Verso, pp. 3–40.

Santos, Boaventura de Sousa, João Arrisacado Nunes and Maria Paula Meneses 2007. 'Introduction: Opening Up the Canon of Knowledge and Recognition of Difference', in Boaventura de Sousa Santos (ed.), *Another Knowledge is Possible: Beyond Northern Epistemologies*. London: Verso, pp. xix–lxii.

Shah, Hemant 2011. *The Production of Modernization: Daniel Lerner, Mass Media, and the Passing of Traditional Society*. Philadelphia, PA: Temple University Press.

Shilliam, Robbie 2006. 'What about Marcus Garvey? Race and the Transformation of Sovereignty Debate', *Review of International Studies* 32 (3): 379–400.

—(ed.) 2011. *International Relations and Non-Western Thought: Imperialism, Colonialism and Investigations of Global Modernity*. London: Routledge.

Silva, Denise Ferreira da 2007. *Toward a Global Idea of Race*. Minneapolis, MN: University of Minneapolis Press.

Singh, Yogendra 1979. 'Constraints, Contradictions, and Interdisciplinary Orientations: The Indian Context', *International Social Science Journal* 31 (1): 114–22.

Sinha, Vineeta 2003. 'Decentring Social Sciences in Practice through Individual Acts and Choices', *Current Sociology* 51 (1): 7–26.

Sitas, Ari 2006. 'The African Renaissance Challenge and Sociological Reclamations in the South', *Current Sociology* 54 (3): 357–80.

Smith, Dennis 1991. *The Rise of Historical Sociology*. Philadelphia, PA: Temple University Pres.

Spivak, Gayatri Chakravorty 1988. 'Can the Subaltern Speak?', in Cary Nelson and Lawrence Grossberg (eds), *Marxism and the Interpretation of Culture*. Chicago, IL: University of Illinois Press, pp. 271–316.

—1990. 'Post-structuralism, Marginality, Postcoloniality and Value', in Peter Collier and Helga Geyer-Ryan (eds), *Literary Theory Today*. Cambridge: Polity Press, 219–44.

Subrahmanyam, Sanjay 1997. 'Connected Histories: Notes towards a Reconfiguration of Early Modern Eurasia', *Modern Asian Studies* 31 (3): 735–62.

—2005a. *Explorations in Connected Histories: Mughals and Franks*. Oxford: Oxford University Press.

—2005b. *Explorations in Connected Histories: From the Tagus to the Ganges.* Oxford: Oxford University Press.

Sztompka, Piotr 2011. 'Another Sociological Utopia', *Contemporary Sociology* 40 (4): 388–96.

Tageldin, Shaden M. 2014. 'The Place of Africa, in Theory: Pan-Africanism, Postcolonialism, Beyond', *Journal of Historical Sociology* 26 (3): tba.

Tipps, Dean C. 1973. 'Modernization Theory and the Comparative Study of Societies: A Critical Perspective', *Comparative Studies in Society and History* 15 (2): 199–226.

Tooze, Adam 2013. 'Empires at War', *New Left Review* 79 (January–February): 129–39.

Trouillot, Michel-Rolph 1991. 'Anthropology and the Savage Slot: The Poetics and Politics of Otherness', in Richard G. Fox (ed.), *Recapturing Anthropology: Working in the Present.* Santa Fe, NM: School of American Research Press, pp. 17–44.

—1995. *Silencing the Past: Power and the Production of History.* Boston, MA: Beacon Press.

—2003. *Global Transformation: Anthropology and the Modern World.* Basingstoke: Palgrave Macmillan.

Vázquez, Rolando 2011. 'Translation as Erasure: Thoughts on Modernity's Epistemic Violence', *Journal of Historical Sociology* 24 (1): 27–44.

Wagner, Peter 2001. *Theorizing Modernity: Inescapability and Attainability in Social Theory.* London: Sage.

Walby, Sylvia 2009. *Globalization and Inequalities: Complexity and Contested Modernities.* London: Sage.

Wallerstein, Immanuel 1974a. *The Modern World-System*, Volume 1: *Capitalist Agriculture and the Origins of the European World-Economy in the Sixteenth Century.* New York: Academic Press.

—1974b. 'Dependence in an Interdependent World: The Limited Possibilities of Transformation within the Capitalist World Economy', *African Studies Review* 17 (1): 1–26.

—1979. *The Capitalist World-Economy: Essays.* Cambridge: Cambridge University Press.

—1980. *The Modern World-System*, Volume 2: *Mercantilism and the Consolidation of the European World-Economy, 1600–1750.* New York: Academic Press.

—2001. *Unthinking Social Science: The Limits of Nineteenth-Century Paradigms.* Second edition with a new Preface. Philadelphia, PA: Temple University Press.

—2011a [1989]. *The Modern World-System*, Volume 3: *The Second Era of Great Expansion of the Capitalist World-Economy, 1730s–1840s*. Berkeley, CA: University of California Press.

—2011b. *The Modern World-System*, Volume 4: *Centrist Liberalism Triumphant, 1789–1914*. Berkeley, CA: University of California Press.

Wallerstein, Immanuel *et al.* 1996. *Open the Social Sciences: Report of the Gulbenkian Commission on the Restructuring of the Social Sciences.* Stanford, CA: Stanford University Press.

Walsh, Catherine E. 2002. 'The (Re)articulation of Political Subjectivities and Colonial Difference in Ecuador Reflections on Capitalism and the Geopolitics of Knowledge', *Nepantla: Views from South* 3 (1): 61–97.

Weber, Max 1930. *The Protestant Ethic and the Spirit of Capitalism*, translated by Talcott Parsons. London: George Allen & Unwin.

Weinstein, Barbara 2005. 'History without a Cause? Grand Narratives, World History, and the Postcolonial Dilemma', *International Review of Social History* 50 (1): 71–93.

Wittrock, Bjorn 1998. 'Early Modernities: Varieties and Transitions', *Daedalus* 127 (3): 19–40.

Wolf, Eric R. 1997 [1982]. *Europe and the People without History*. Berkeley, CA: University of California Press.

Wynter, Sylvia 2003. 'Unsettling the Coloniality of Being/Power/Truth/Freedom: Towards the Human, After Man, Its Overrepresetnation – An Argument', *CR: The New Centennial Review* 3 (3): 257–337.

Yonay, Yuval P. 1998. *The Struggle over the Soul of Economics: Institutionalist and Neoclassical Economists in America between the Wars*. Princeton, NJ: Princeton University Press.

Index